2

THE CUTTING EDGE

Series Editors:
Susan Weil, Head of Higher Education Development and Fellow in Organizational Learning at the Office for Public Management, and Visting Lecturer for the Centre for Higher Education Studies, University of London. *Malcolm Tight*, Senior Lecturer in Continuing Education, University of Warwick.

This series deals with critical issues and significant developments in continuing education, focusing on its impact on higher education.

Current titles in the series:

Tom Bourner *et al.*: *Part-Time Students and their Experience of Higher Education*
Chris Duke: *The Learning University*
David Smith and Michael Saunders: *Other Routes: Part-Time Higher Education Policy*

The Learning University

Towards a New Paradigm?

CHRIS DUKE

The Society for Research into Higher Education
& Open University Press

Published by SRHE and
Open University Press
Celtic Court
22 Ballmoor
Buckingham
MK18 1XW

and

1900 Frost Road, Suite 101
Bristol, PA 19007, USA

First published 1992

A catalogue record of this book is available from the British Library

Library of Congress Cataloging-in-Publication Data

Duke, C. (Christopher)
    The learning university: towards a new paradigm? / Chris Duke.
        p.   cm. — (Cutting edge)
    Includes bibliographical references and index.
      ISBN 0-335-15654-1   ISBN 0-335-15653-3 (pbk.)
      1. Education, Higher — Great Britain.   I. Title.   II. Series:
    Cutting edge (Buckingham, England)
    LA637.D77   1992
    378.41 — dc20   91-44438
                                                                  CIP

Typeset by Graphicraft Typesetters Limited, Hong Kong
Printed in Great Britain by St Edmundsbury Press,
Bury St Edmunds, Suffolk

Contents

Series Editor's Introduction

The Cutting Edge series was established to examine how developments related to access and continuing education in their broadest sense are throwing into sharper relief fundamental questions about higher education itself. In other words, how is what is happening at what some might call the margins in fact transforming the mainstream?

The book uses as a starting-point the 1991–2 to 1994–5 bids made by the universities to the Universities Funding Council (UFC) for funding generally. Continuing education (CE) is often, as the author argues, a 'conduit for the entry of new ideas and new language into the teaching life of the university'. It was therefore fitting that these bids provided the means for testing the water of the new UFC regime.

The author offers a thorough and interesting analysis of these data, against a political background of discontinuity and uncertainty. He relates trends and issues evident in the bids to current debates and developments in adult, continuing and higher education – a task for which his own background makes him well suited. He provides a comprehensive picture of the terrain: from questions about the HE curriculum and how it is to be understood and delivered in future (propelled by, for example, credit accumulation and transfer, resource constraints, the influence of non-traditional and non-standard students and projected expansion of numbers) to quality, resource and management issues.

The outcomes of these endeavours alone would have made a suitable publication for the series. But, the author goes further than this. He clearly demonstrates how the nature, aims and objectives of universities as portrayed through these particular bids are 'sharply at variance with what has come to be regarded as the traditional model of elite teaching and frontier research'. But he also uses the firm scaffolding of his analysis of the bids as a vehicle for illuminating questions that are far bolder.

Relentlessly yet thoughtfully, the author questions how clear and purposeful universities are about shifting their energies into continuing education alongside initial education, and just what this will entail. In doing so, he nudges the reader towards a deeper understanding of how and why the very idea of the university is being implicitly transformed, because of but also in spite of current political agendas. He examines the pressures on universities to become more responsive to change within society as a whole, and to the needs and aspirations of a broader base of learners. He speaks of the need for a 'reallocation of educational effort to promote learning throughout life'. But he provocatively and rightfully questions whether such developments can be kept tightly reined at the margins of a front-end traditional image of the university, never really touching the academic tribes' and territories' (Becher 1989) taken for granted ways of thinking, behaving and attaching value.

The author also examines current notions of managerialism and efficiency. He suggests that pressures in this direction may be combining to centralize the development and management of continuing education. However, as they are currently understood, they may work against government aims for expansion and continuing education.

His metaphor of paradigm shift is therefore most apt. Our most implicit and fundamental sets of beliefs and values, and how we assume they relate to each other, whether we speak about management, quality or resources, are all demanding reconceptualization in light of current and projected trends. Old criteria may be fundamentally at odds with new visions, and therefore have limited validity. At the very least, they can no longer be taken for granted. Moreover, he suggests that those universities,

> that adhere to their traditional aims and objectives in the coming years will experience a lot more internal grinding and jarring as the nature and meaning of the new paradigm are experienced and become clearer through that experience.

The author offers his own thoughts on how universities can evolve within a new paradigm, accommodating traditional strengths and values as well as new missions and visions. In particular, he speaks of aligning the service mission of universities alongside its commitments to teaching and research. He elaborates an image of the university as a lifelong resource centre: a fluidly bounded place for continual learning and renewal by all who are involved with the institution, highly valued as a resource by politicans and the wider community.

How to translate such an image from rhetoric to reality poses no end of challenges. As Duke points out, slippage between institutional policies and departmental behaviour can be substantial. The challenge of expanding systems thus raises new and profound questions about the structure and management of the system. For example, how can loyalties to access, lifelong learning, and institutional missions and visions be nurtured alongside loyalties to professional autonomy, collegiality, one's disciplines, and the wider international academic community?

The author introduces the idea of organizational learning – a notion that is gaining currency outside HE. He offers a much welcomed exploration of its explanatory power for HE. For traditional notions of staff development may also be too firmly lodged within a paradigm beyond which we now must move in order to create a non-elitist system of lifelong provision.

It is not the newness of such ideas that makes this book so distinctive. Rather, it is how the author joins up the analysis of data to wider questions about the contradictory contours of current experience and future possibility in HE.

This book is thus not only timely and fresh. It embodies the very essence of *The Cutting Edge* series' intention.

Susan Weil

Preface

Do universities really learn? Organizations as well as individuals *can* learn. They can take in and use new information, adapt their identities, purposes and priorities to new environments and circumstances, change and survive – or, perhaps, fail to learn and adapt, atrophy and die. Universities are institutions dedicated to learning and the furtherance of understanding, so this book has a dual focus: to examine how far universities are learning, changing and adapting; and to ask how this connects with their amplification of learning through the broadening academic communities which, as lifelong learning centres, they may become.

The 1990s and the approaching millennium make bold headlines, with slogans about Access and Accountability, Adaptability and Appraisal, and on through the alphabet. Is this a new era in higher education? Or just an old familiar story: the *realpolitik* of bending with the wind, while the essentials remain unaltered, another case of '*plus ça change*' – a French phrase for a peculiarly British phenomenon? Are universities becoming different kinds of organizations and institutions with a new kind of mission as we approach the twenty-first century?

This is a particularly British story, but its essential themes are universal and abiding. Discourse about the nature and purposes – the idea – of a university persists in modern times (Newman 1852; Allen 1988; Barnett 1990), yet it is said to be under-conceptualized, studied too little (Trow 1989; Tight 1991). Is the subject best addressed in terms of the essence of 'the university'; in terms of the characteristics and needs of modern – and in the West economics-driven and secular – societies; or empirically, 'scientifically', by describing and analysing what universities now are and now do?

The answer is all three. 'The university' is made and remade by new pressures and needs in new times and circumstances, as new societies emerge from the old. 'Philosophical' statements reflect these needs and circumstances. They tend to be selectively historical, drawing on a preferred period and mode to uncover the essential university. There is an authoritative innocence about studying empirically what universities 'are'. It is not just that selection, comparison and interpretation of data are problematic, arbitrary and subjective. The very process of study holds up a chosen and distorting mirror. There is no need to draw conclusions as such. The inquiry becomes inescapably part of the subject matter. Describing what *is* unavoidably suggests what *should be*, and may be a factor in making it.

This book pretends to no such innocence. Its author, working for twenty-five years from bases in university continuing education, is committed to action no less than to analysis. The book is written from a firm belief in a learning society as a condition of human survival. Universities, at the pinnacles of the world's mass education systems, play a highly influential, if indirect, role in the quality of individuals' learning throughout these systems. Admissions criteria press back on and distort the school curriculum. The signals sent out by universities' behaviour can be more important than their direct demands and contributions. With them the creation of learning societies or its frustration in important part rests.

At the heart of this proposition are the different universities themselves. How and how far are they 'learning organizations'? How do they adapt to new circumstances? The quintessence of organized intelligence formally dedicated to its own and other noble ends, universities have an abiding fascination for the inquiring mind. The stream of books about universities will not dry up, although how far they affect universities' evolution and behaviour is another matter. How far universities may, as key teaching and learning institutions, practically speaking adopt the new paradigm of lifelong learning is what this book is about.

Lifelong learning offers a window through which to look at the role and future of universities. Looking through that window we will not see for certain what the university of the early twenty-first century will be like, but we enjoy an unusual perspective: a point of view different from that adopted by studies which start from older concerns with undergraduate teaching and research. Continuing education (CE) in the broad sense that it has come to be used is at the cutting edge in higher education – a Trojan horse, perhaps, to smuggle in change.

There was keen concern in the late 1980s that falling birth rates would drive universities to seek new 'markets' of student clienteles in order to survive. The star of continuing education, it seemed, was rising. We need not take too seriously cynical, sceptical or simply sad observations about the fizzing out of the 'demographic timebomb' (Smithers and Robinson 1989), the feeling that because there are still plenty of youngsters coming forward for university places this will 'let universities off the hook'. The issues confronting universities and discussed in the following pages run wider and deeper than such perturbations in the demographic profile of the nation.

This book tells a story about the way British universities perceived their development in the stories they told to the Universities Funding Council (UFC) at the beginning of the 1990s. Very shortly, following publication of the higher education White Paper in 1991 (Clarke *et al.* 1991), the 'binary line' separating British universities from polytechnics will be removed, and polytechnics will adopt the name university. Then a new set of questions about the meaning, mission and diversity of universities will arise. The polytechnics are not part of this story, however. Nor is that very distinctive university exclusively dedicated to continuing education, the Open University, which has hitherto been funded by the DES.

I set out, then, to examine the extent to which and the means by which universities are looking to become centres for lifelong learning, other than in offering more 'short course CE'. I explore how far the concepts and requirements for institution-wide continuing education have been identified and built into institutional planning. The book is arranged as follows.

The first chapter, in considering the idea of a new paradigm, calls attention to assumptions by and about universities, some of them hitherto taken for granted but now being seriously challenged. It calls attention also to the changing context of universities – the environment in which they function and on which they depend for survival via an agreed definition of their *raison d'être*. It considers, too, processes of change and resistance to change within the university, and explains the sources for the story told in the rest of the book.

There follows a consideration of the new language which has invaded education and begun to enter the universities. How far have they learned, embraced, co-opted or perhaps so far ignored it? What are its implications, if taken seriously? The third chapter then considers what may be new about the mission statements, aims and objectives of universities, with an eye particularly to the language of lifelong learning, and continuing and recurrent education.

The next chapter asks how far the purposes of continuing education are being assumed and planned for by means of new structures and new arrangements within established university teaching, rather than in an area separately identified as continuing education. What about new principles of curriculum design and their application: the modularization of degree courses, the wider implementation of credit transfer arrangements, and new forms of partnership beyond and even within the university? This leads to a discussion of the compatibility, and the tension, between the more established and the less familiar, so-called non-traditional, forms of activity. How persistent and exclusive is the eighteen-plus, pre-experience or front-end-loaded model of education? How firmly are university teachers wedded to this initial mode of education? Is there room for, and useful interaction with, newer clienteles?

Access is considered as a major contemporary theme in the development or reform of higher education. What do we understand to be the acceptably successful student? Much is heard about performance indicators and measures, about standards, quality, accountability and appraisal. The basic currency is, however, commonly taken for granted in a quite narrow, unreflecting and ahistorical sense. Success may be about adapting to new needs and clienteles, and fashioning new measures, rather than simply recalibrating measures which are well known and well worn.

The penultimate chapter is about staff development, which can be thought of as 'internal continuing education' within each university. Is there a will to place equal trust, and resources, in the continuing education medicine increasingly prescribed for others? If so, does this suggest any shift among universities towards becoming, more deliberately, learning organizations?

Universities have expressed, to the Universities Funding Council and in other ways, their aspirations to provide continuing education and to operate more like lifelong learning centres. The concluding chapter asks how much further such changes might run; whether there really is emerging an alternative paradigm; how up to date our perceptions of the universities may in fact be. The membership of the 'academic community', both faculty and students, is rapidly changing – more rapidly than shared perception and agreement as to what the academic community now is, and whom it now includes. Possibly the university which we argue about has already ceased to exist. On the other hand, if we recognize the new reality more clearly this may make it easier to accept the change, and in the process more gently to usher in university lifelong learning centres.

A note on terms

Lifelong learning is the key concept from which policy propositions about recurrent education derive. *Recurrent education* means alternation of education with employment, leisure and other activities throughout the lifespan instead of completing all formal education before entering fully into adult life. *Continuing education* (CE) is a category of provision to which policy-makers in many countries increasingly pay attention – the later education in whatever form of those who have left initial full-time education and embarked on adult life and usually work.

Other terms will be explained if this seems necessary as they arise. Most important is *lifelong learning*. Learning takes place throughout life and also 'life-wide' – that is to say, in many places and circumstances, not just at school and college. Alan Tough studied adults' learning projects in Canada twenty years ago, and the idea of self-directed learning is still being refined and exploited in studies germane to building a 'learning society' (Tough 1971, 1982; Calder 1989, Farnes 1990).

Resources deliberately allocated to support learning comprise education budgets. Modern societies invest massively in education, unequally between and within nations. Generally they favour the young and the richer over the older and the poorer. *Recurrent education* is a policy proposition to support lifelong learning (OECD 1973; Houghton and Richardson 1974; Schuller and Megarry 1979; Duke 1982). It affords a policy framework for re-allocating education resources throughout life in place of the dominant 'front-end-loading' paradigm suited to more static 'traditional' societies. Universities are still taken to be essentially about initial, pre-experience, rather than recurrent education.

Lifelong learning is the key concept, recurrent education the policy proposition. *Continuing education* (CE) is the broad administrative category now normally used to refer to all education following a break from full-time schooling. In this book it encompasses all forms of university (liberal) adult education or (L)AE; the various forms of occupationally oriented refresher and updating courses known by such acronyms as CPD, CVE, PEVE and PICKUP; and the introduction of older students into the regular degree and other award-bearing programmes of the 'mainstream university'. The very term and category can become a cage for our thinking, since for some, CE still connotes no more than separately provided 'short courses'. In this book we ask (a) how much effort is shifting from initial to continuing education, and (b) how clearly and deliberately universities are making the change.

List of Abbreviations

AAU	Academic Audit Unit (of the CVCP)
ACACE	Advisory Council for Adult and Continuing Education
ACRG	Access Courses Recognition Group (of CNAA/CVCP)
AE	adult education
AFE	advanced further education
APEL	accreditation of prior experiential learning
APHE	Association for Part-time Higher Education
ASDT	academic staff development and training
AUT	Association of University Teachers
AVA	Authorised Validating Agency (of the CNAA/CVCP ACRG)
BTEC	Business and Technician Education Council
CAT	credit accumulation and transfer
CBI	Confederation of British Industry
CDP	Committee of Directors of Polytechnics
CE	continuing education
CER	Continuing Education Record
CET	continuing education and training
CIHE	Council for Industry and Higher Education
CNAA	Council for National Academic Awards
CPD	continuing professional development
CPE	continuing professional education
CTEC	(Australian) Commonwealth Tertiary Education Commission
CVCP	Committee of Vice-Chancellors and Principals
CVE(T)	continuing vocational education (and training)
DES	Department of Education and Science
DTI	Department of Trade and Industry
EHE	Enterprise in Higher Education
EMD	extramural department
FAST	Forum for Access Studies
FE	further education

FESC	Further Education Staff College (now The Staff College)
FEU	Further Education Unit
FHE	further and higher education
FTE	full-time equivalent (student)
GCE	General Certificate of Education
GCSE	General Certificate of Secondary Education
HE	higher education
HEI	higher education institution
HMI	Her Majesty's Inspectorate
HRD	human resource development
IGDS	Integrated Graduate Development Scheme
INSET	in-service education of teachers
LAE	liberal adult education
MBA	Master of Business Administration
MSC	Manpower Services Commission (subsequently TA, then TEED)
NAB	National Advisory Board
NAFE	non-advanced further education
NCVQ	National Council for Vocational Qualifications
NGO	non-governmental organization
NIACE	National Institute of Adult Continuing Education
NSE	non-standard entry
OECD	Organisation for Economic Cooperation and Development
OU	Open University
PACE	Polytechnics Association for Continuing Education
PCFC	Polytechnics and Colleges Funding Council
PEVE	post-experience vocational education
PI	performance indicator
PICKUP	Professional Industrial and Commercial Updating
PM	performance measure
PCAS	Polytechnics Central Admissions System
RB	Responsible Body (DES funding for LAE, terminated 1989)
RDA	(PICKUP) Regional Development Agent (ARDA: Assistant RDA)
RSA	Royal Society for the Encouragement of Arts, Manufactures and Commerce
SIACE	Scottish Institute of Adult Continuing Education
SCUTREA	Standing Conference on University Teaching and Research in the Education of Adults
SDTU	Staff Development and Training Unit (of the CVCP)
SDO/SDU	staff development officer/unit
SDTO/SDTU	staff development and training officer/unit
SRHE	Society for Research into Higher Education
SSR	staff–student ratio
TA	Training Agency (formerly Manpower Services Commission, then Training Commission and from late 1990 the

	Training, Enterprise and Education Directorate of the Department of Employment Group)
TAFE	technical and further education (in Australia)
TC	Training Commission (previously MSC, later TA, then TEED)
TEC	Training and Enterprise Council
TEED	Training, Enterprise and Education Directorate of the Department of Employment Group (previously MSC, TC and TA)
THES	*Times Higher Education Supplement*
UCACE	Universities Council for Adult and Continuing Education
UCCA	Universities Central Council on Admissions
UDACE	Unit for the Development of Adult Continuing Education
UFC	Universities Funding Council
UGC	University Grants Committee
UNESCO	United Nations Educational, Scientific and Cultural Organisation
USR	Universities Statistical Record
WEA	Workers' Educational Association

1 | Old Assumptions and New Practices

A new paradigm?

Is it helpful to speak of a new paradigm of the university – a new way of seeing and understanding? Has a new idea of the university emerged from the chrysalis of the old, needing but a name for recognition? Do prevailing old assumptions obscure new practices? Does naming alter the reality – for there may be much in a name? It has been said that a rose by any other name would smell as sweet – but changing the terms, fostering new discourse, acknowledging a new paradigm, can in themselves assist a shift of values and assumptions which makes new practices more than superficial. Conversely, is playing with new words a form of protectionism – gestures of change to mask an abiding dominant reality?

Metaphor can be a handy way to consider paradigm shift. In this book various metaphors are employed from time to time. The one preferred in the title is 'the learning organization' – an organization that both learns and fosters learning.

Assumptions about universities

However varied the functions of universities in the modern world, they retain their central role as providers of post-secondary education for ... secondary school leavers .... The millions of young men and women who, term after term, semester after semester, have registered and re-registered on campuses around the world for first degrees and diplomas have given the modern university its distinctive appearance, architecture, and character.

OECD 1986: 39

If universities remain centrally providers of education for school leavers they are also now centrally about research, although they have not always been important as centres for the creation of new knowledge; some societies look to other kinds of institutions for much of their research effort (Tight 1991).

The need for reappraisal is noted by the OECD. Thus, in 1983:

the crisis of higher education is not merely one of public confidence
vis-a-vis the performance of higher education; it is also ... an internal
crisis of purpose, that is one which touches the very nature of individual
institutions, their roles and functions and their place in the total higher
education system. In this, a reappraisal of the special position of the
university appeared as crucial.

OECD 1983: 55

And three years later:

The main dangers to the future of the universities in OECD countries
are seen to be 'not so much institutional extinction ... as failure to
balance clarity and control of missions and objectives on the one hand,
with on the other, freedom to develop new purposes and activities;
failure to promote and give status to high-level discussion about
wholes ... rather than parts.'

OECD 1986: 1

Universities around the world have much in common, despite great differences. Some are virtually branches of the civil service yet at the same time
centres and flashpoints for radical or revolutionary political action – as they
were, very briefly, in Western societies at the end of the 1960s. There are
common beliefs about the nature, values and abiding value of 'the university'. Vice-chancellors, rectors and principals gathered from all over the world
to celebrate the 900th birthday of the University of Bologna. An international academic freemasonry finds expression through institutional leaders' meetings (gatherings of the International Association of Universities, the
Commonwealth Universities' Association and the European rectors) and
through gatherings of Becher's (1989) 'academic tribes' in subject-specific
international conferences. These are powerful forces for continuity.

At the same time industrialized nations share a 'macro-environment':
economic upturn or recession; a swing to the political right; common demographic trends; technological obsolescence and the shortening half-life of
much knowledge. The OECD, through its Education Committee work and
through the Centre for Educational Research and Innovation (CERI), monitors the more tangible elements of these changes and their impact on (higher) education.

A subtler cultural conflict also exists: between the long time horizons of the
university ethos and the 'culture of the microsecond' which compels stock
exchanges to install circuit breakers against information technology-induced
disaster. Ministers of state exhort vice-chancellors to sell off their real estate
as a short-term check to insolvency. Polytechnics, newly endowed with property transferred from local authorities on 'vesting day' (1 April 1989), are
exhorted to operate like real estate barons; to borrow, invest and realize (see,
for instance, *THES* 2 January 1991). More congenial to an older (is it also to
prove a more abiding?) idea of a university and the custody of its assets, an
Oxford college bursar annually walks the boundaries of each of his college's
widely scattered estates as if ritually to be assured that they are still there.

The university and higher education

Our subject is continuity and change in the British universities as (excepting the Open University) these are identified in 1991. A commonly accepted rough categorization of universities (see below) is generally acknowledged in terms of their history, style, status and size. It masks great diversity between institutions in each category. Looked at from the United States, from Germany or from the Philippines, the UK universities are remarkably homogeneous, the OU apart. Shift the focus and each institution appears proudly unique. The system is distinctly elite: hard to enter, expensive per full-time student, efficient in terms of completion rates. On the other hand universities vie with one another to attract the best prospective students. While they look similar from a distance, each stresses uniqueness and special strength to value and sell itself.

The larger higher education system is also quite exclusive compared with North American, European and indeed most other systems. Those who enter a degree programme are expected to complete it in the minimum time. Programmes are mostly specialized, requiring students to advance a long way on the narrow front into which they were launched by a narrow upper secondary education. Most are still, typically, a preparation for the academic career to which only a tiny minority of students actually proceed. Higher education is defined by level. It is not merely a later stage, for Britain lacks the concept of a tertiary stage of education.

In the United States the term higher education (HE) embraces all work at the tertiary stage. British educational administration distinguishes advanced from non-advanced work in the further education (FE) sector (AFE and NAFE). Thus some HE work sits outside the HE sector and within FE. It has been suggested that all this should be tidied up, and HE work removed from FE (Perry 1990). A stronger groundswell – both principled and pragmatic – favours weakening or even abolishing the FE–HE divide, and moving towards a more open lattice-type FHE, or tertiary, system (see, for example, several *THES* leaders during 1990). This might be post-secondary (eighteen plus) or post-compulsory (sixteen plus). The 1991 White Paper removing FE from local authority control (DES 1991) may sharpen this debate and precipitate new FHE relationships.

In this book, while concentrating on institutions now funded via the UFC – the 'universities proper' – I also recognize that categories and boundaries are changing fast, perhaps dissolving. Such change promises dramatically to alter our idea of what a university is and should be.

Universities and continuing education

An overarching concept here is *lifelong learning*. The need to learn throughout life is seen as vital in the world of practical affairs as well as being recognized intellectually (Faure 1972), as publications and pronouncements of bodies like the Confederation of British Industry (CBI) and the Council for Industry and Higher Education (CIHE) demonstrate. Learning is a normal human activity which occurs throughout life. Realizing this has had a liberating effect on our understanding of human potential (see, for instance, Cross 1981). If learning throughout life is vital to the individual, so too is it to the organization and to the whole society. The idea of a learning society (Commission on Post-Secondary Education 1972; Husen 1974) and a learning organization is becoming more familiar. We may prefer terms like 'organization development', but we speak without discomfort about institutional memory (and see, for example, Argyris and Schon 1978). Why not a learning university?

Continuing education is at the cutting edge as universities become more fully 'learning organizations'. It has not always been so. The traditional term and means for providing distinctly adult education has been the extramural department (EMD), somewhat cut off from its parent institution and valuing mainly liberal ('adult education') over occupationally oriented (continuing vocational education) work. This has not only kept EMDs off the cutting edge of their parent institutions. It has also helped to perpetuate a dichotomy between the liberal and the vocational which perhaps runs deeper in British history and culture than in any other society. It is at the root of the social divisiveness and educational inadequacy which much preoccupy historians and other analysts of British society (Roderick and Stephens 1984; Stephens 1989; Cassels 1990; Moser 1991).

Newman's idea of a university has exercised a powerful hold over the adult education tradition in universities. There is ritual obeisance to Newman in liberal adult education circles. Others concerned with the higher education mainstream may refer to him, but to different effect. Thus Robert Jackson, at a Newman Centenary Conference, said of Newman's analysis:

> It does actually indicate the right direction: towards a focus on what current jargon describes as the 'personal transferable skills' which should be promoted in every educational process.
>
> Jackson 1990: 11

An unintended consequence of the university extramural tradition embracing Newman's Idea has been extramural departments' isolation, referred to above. Some tended to box themselves off from their parent institutions by becoming keepers of Newman's Holy Grail – with unwitting disdainful superiority over 'internal' colleagues. This psychological distance made it harder to contribute to university debate about the priorities and mission of the university as a whole. Newman's idea of a university was actually a quite modest one: excluding research but

> not an aloof, detached, or cloistered and sequestered place: it is 'hemmed in by public thoroughfares' – situated firmly within the world, and interacting vigorously at every point with it.
>
> Jackson 1990: 20

Adhering to Newman and the liberal tradition built conflict into the identity of the EMDs. They have been torn between commitment to social

Table 1.1 Changing nomenclature of continuing education departments

	1980–1	*1988–9*
Extramural	19	6
Adult education	14	11
Continuing education	10	33
Other title	4	8
No distinct unit	7	3

purpose (if not action) and educational purism, according to which 'the debate's the thing'. It is often unclear whether the extramural tradition represented the political cutting edge of university education or its most innocent and detached component. Either way, the liberal adult education tradition, in claiming to represent the pure essence of the liberal university, largely denied itself effective dialogue with the universities over any wider re-definition of university mission.

The names of university departments to do with CE have, however, been changing rapidly – a sign of a paradigm shift here, ahead of the universities themselves? There is considerable diversity of names, revealing not only rapid change but also instability and lack of confidence: a desire both to value tradition and to be up to date. The diversity, and the rapidity of change, appears bewildering, but there is a pattern. The annual reports of the Universities Council for Adult and Continuing Education (UCACE) show what happened during the 1980s. Table 1.1 simply aggregates the words used in the names (some double-barrelled) in each of these two years by the fifty or so member universities.

What is the problem?

What do universities see the job as being, as distinct from what to call it?

The UFC grasped continuing education more firmly than did its predecessor, the UGC, allocating some forty million pounds to CE for academic year 1991–2 (compared with a few million for PICKUP pump-priming from the UGC plus about six million pounds of DES/RB money until 1988–9). On the other hand, as is explained in Chapter 3, the UGC working party on continuing education defined CE as including any form of education 're-sumed after an interval following the end of continuous initial education' (UGC 1984b). UFC CE funding is more restricted: it excludes part-time and other mature age degree students. While providing better support for (non-degree) continuing education it thus continues to separate it off from the mainstream of university teaching.

This book is concerned with mainstream CE, and the extent to which it heralds a new paradigm of the university, rather than just with separately identified and funded CE of the 'short course' variety.

'Academic drift' describes the behaviour of educational institutions which become preoccupied with teaching at higher academic levels than was originally intended for them, neglecting their initial primary teaching mission. The same term could be applied to universities when preoccupation with research displaces energies from teaching. The pressure of the UGC's and now the UFC's comparative evaluation of research in universities (known as the 'research selectivity exercise') has been added to an older stress within universities upon research and publications as a main criterion for promotion – 'publish or perish'. The 'idea of a university' immortalized by John Henry Newman in the mid-nineteenth century concerned an *educational* ideal. Research really did not feature as such. We are here concerned with research only insofar as it determines identity and mission, barring a wider definition of scope and mission to encompass CE within a recurrent education paradigm.

In principle there should be no problem. CE is entirely compatible with research and the generation of new knowledge. Indeed it may often sit more easily with research than does undergraduate teaching. Often adults can contribute more to the advancement of knowledge than can young people straight from school who are studying for a first degree.

In practice there is a problem. Its presented form is pressure of time. Few university teachers and scholars, in my experience, argue that CE is unimportant or inappropriate to a university. They do remind you of the pressures, both individual and institutional, to do research. Less explicitly, for here we are in the realm of assumptions, they take it for granted that their contract means teaching undergraduate and graduate students; and that the former are, normally and essentially, young men and women straight from school. CE students, both 'short course' students not working towards a degree and 'non-traditional' degree students – those of mature age, those on a part-time track – are assumed to be ancillary: more marginal, of lower priority. They are not the essential business of the university, not part of that 'idea of a university' which for the carriers of the cultural tradition, the mainstream academics in their 'academic tribes and territories' (Becher 1989), naturally comes to mind. Is the British university of the 1990s bringing older students and what the Americans call the 'community service' third leg of mission and identity into balance with (young people's) teaching and with research?

A sense of purpose, continuity and conservation is part of the idea of a university. This is latently inimical to continuing education; for it sits with the tradition of a residential, almost monastic, period of education for young men and now, quite recently in terms of the history of British universities, for young women. Reflection through study combines with non-responsibility. This deeply ingrained 'finishing school' assumption contrasts with the more typically American 'service station' notion of a university. The service model is also commonly sought in the development context of the Third World – although here too it often competes with the socialization, the laying on of hands, that makes universities so powerful in small elite HE systems where a university degree is a mark of real distinction and a valid ticket to future opportunity.

Writing of the informal curriculum, the OECD maintained in 1986 that 'save in a few highly selective and usually highly self-conscious places, the collegiate ideal has for all practical purposes disappeared'.

> Efforts to influence, let alone control, the personal lives of students have been virtually abandoned. Student culture and the general youth culture are virtually indistinguishable . . . . The concept of the collegiate residential university has been a casualty of expansion.
>
> OECD 1986: 60

In its extreme form the concept of the residential community and its educative experience was valued more highly than the formal curriculum, a valuation shared by many employers. 'The case for providing residence is now largely utilitarian rather than moral. Its educational benefits are no longer so strongly asserted as before' (OECD 1986: 62).

It may be true that the strictly collegiate ideal has been killed by expansion through OECD countries. Yet British universities and British, especially perhaps English, society cling to the idea of going away to university. There is still a coming of age, even though the *in loco parentis* element is much reduced and new rituals may have replaced earlier symbols for the coming of age. I return to this subject in Chapter 5.

'Finishing school' is a relevant and powerful metaphor for two reasons. First, it is a complete contradiction of the idea of recurrent education (RE), according to which people return periodically to formal education for updating, refreshment, etc. It implies the complete, finished person, the 'educated man' [*sic*], fully equipped for life. Secondly, it is costly, being residential. This makes it highly selective, therefore somewhat socially exclusive, and thus inimical to notions of access to mass HE. A logical application of RE and lifelong learning perspectives might go so far as to suggest that the very idea of a degree – a bachelor, master or doctor – is inappropriate to and counterproductive in contemporary society!

The changing environment

Changes in the world at large, particularly in high technology, information-rich, post-industrial societies, constitute an environmental common to all universities. It is an environment in many ways culturally alien to the traditional university, both British and continental European. At the same time it opens up new and large opportunities for universities, and higher education institutions (HEIs) more widely, as the need for highly skilled and frequently updated labour shows itself.

The choice may appear to be between re-definition of mission to respond, through growth and diversification, to these opportunities; and contracting around older core purposes – initial education of a small elite cadre and selective high-level research. This, however, implies more clear, rational and purposeful behaviour than most universities by their very nature can commonly muster (see Allen 1988: 26).

Government has exerted pressure in the form of the Jarratt Report (Jarratt 1985) and subsequent actions. The complex, ambiguous, collegial nature of universities and their goals will probably mean that their directions will continue to be determined erratically: some clear policy decisions; some weakly directed responses to opportunities and pressures in the environment. Reaction may remain commoner than initiation of change. Therefore, rather than choosing between growth and diversification, or more focused concentration around a familiar core, most universities will probably attempt both simultaneously. This will reflect, but only in part, their capacity to 'read' the changing environment. We will see later whether planning statements to the UFC support this proposition.

The immediate environment of British universities, as felt by their senior administrators, is much influenced by the agencies of government. As long as universities rely on the public exchequer for a large part of their income the influence of Treasury and ultimately the Cabinet is decisively important. Ministers of State for Education, and the DES, provide the more immediate political contact and context. The UFC is intended to provide a sharpened form of the arms-length planning and resourcing previously mediated through the UGC. In principle the UFC buys those educational services which it (and the Government for which it acts in this sense) requires of the autonomous universities, providing the price and quality are right.

The Committee of Vice-Chancellors and Principals (CVCP), as the universities' management club, negotiates with Government and the UFC for the universities. It is also a channel for expressing, while mediating, Government will. Hence quality assurance is sought through the CVCP's Academic Audit Unit (AAU), set up in 1990, and also through its Staff Development and Training Unit (SDTU), created a little earlier. CVCP has an ambiguous relationship with the universities, representing as it does 'management', and negotiating with the Association of University Teachers (AUT) as well as with Government. While these are the most central agencies and channels for engaging with Government, universities also have links, and draw resources in return for services, with other Government departments for different teaching and research purposes – Employment, Health, Trade and Industry, Defence and the Home Office, for example – as well as increasingly with the European Community's organs in Brussels.

The national environment of universities also comprises its markets and competitors, especially industry, represented through bodies like the Confederation of British Industry (CBI) and locally, from 1990, the Training and Enterprise Councils (TECs). For the polytechnics the Committee of Directors of Polytechnics (CDP) matches the CVCP. There are also link mechanisms, like the Council for Industry and Higher Education (CIHE). Even before the appearance of the Government White Paper on Higher Education (Clarke *et al.* 1991), foreshadowing the abolition of the binary divide and heralding a post-binary era, polytechnics and universities were increasingly finding that, despite competition built in by Government funding arrangements, they had a common interest in cooperating on several matters of policy.

To this quick sketch of the environment of the university may be added other agencies more specific to continuing education. Within the DES there is the PICKUP operation. Within the Department of Employment is TEED (formerly the TA and before that the MSC). There is the National Institute for Adult Continuing Education (NIACE), and the Unit for the Development of Adult Continuing Education (UDACE), which is merging with the Further Education Unit (FEU). Other significant non-governmental bodies include the Royal Society for the Arts (RSA), which is promoting Capability in higher education (referred to in the next chapter). There are special interest associations like the Association for Part-time Higher Education (APHE) and the Forum for Access Studies (FAST). The Further Education Staff College (FESC) is an active contributor to the FHE policy debate, and has dropped the FE from its name in token of this. Finally the National Council for Vocational Qualifications (NCVQ) is seeking to rationalize, standardize and modernize all vocational qualifications. It is slowly moving into the line of vision first of those in university CE and later, no doubt, of universities' central administrations.

This list could be much extended, especially by reference to changes affecting schools and local education authorities, from the 1988 Education Reform Act to the White Paper on Further Education (DES 1991). Enough has been said to convey a sense of the unstable and confusing environment of universities even in this limited, mainly bureaucratic, professional and quasi-governmental sense. The economic, socio-cultural and information technology environment is as richly complex and fast-changing; its changes interact in unpredictable ways one part with another. The 'causal texture' of the environment is hard to read. Yet understanding its nature is important for institutional management (Emery 1969: Chapter 12). How well are universities equipped for this task?

The Universities Funding Council

Among all these factors, the Universities Funding Council stands out as most directly influential. It came into being in April 1989, made its broad aims known (UFC 1989a), and quickly came to be felt within university continuing education, calling for bids from universities for CE funds for the academic year 1990–1 These funds were allocated early in 1990. Meanwhile the UK universities in their entirety were set the task of producing planning statements and bidding for funds for the four academic years 1991–2 to 1994–5. Planning statements and offers, as they were called, were to be submitted in June 1990 for a decision to be announced in February 1991 (UFC 1989b). In other words, universities were to indicate how much degree teaching and how much CE they would offer to do, at what price, within a general planning framework.

For degree teaching, unlike CE, the Council issued guide prices for different subject areas. That is to say, the Council indicated how much it considered it proper to pay to teach a full-time student in the different subject areas, and invited universities to offer to teach so many students in each subject area at, or below, this 'guide price'. After the bids (or offers) and planning statements came in to the UFC and had been analysed by panels of advisers, there followed a period of confusion and acute consternation late in 1990. The Council announced that bids were insufficiently competitive. It was said that universities had arranged a price-fixing cartel. Therefore student numbers, and with them funds, would be allocated for one year only (this decision was later partly reversed). Before the outcome of the main bids was known, examination of bids for CE having gone ahead uncomplicated by guide prices, the CE result for the whole period was announced separately and a little earlier in 1991 than the main outcome.

It is fitting that CE, as so often, was the leading edge for innovation – in this case testing the water of the UFC regime. The new system added to universities' 'environmental perturbation' rather than stabilizing anything. There was rapid turnover of both senior and junior Education Ministers: Baker, McGregor, then Clarke, at the most senior level, with matching change beneath them – Walden, Jackson, then Howarth for higher education, and other ministerial changes affecting some aspects of university CE. This amplified the sense of discontinuity and uncertainty.

The sixty-six planning statements made by British university institutions to the Funding Council for the four years to 1995 provide the main database and story-line for this book. They come from thirty-six English universities, the federal University of Wales with its six constituent colleges, eight Scottish universities and two universities in Northern Ireland (which are included in the UFC process though treated differently in some detail). The federal University of London includes fourteen colleges which each prepared separate bids. The Open University, still then funded by the DES, was excluded. I will refer loosely and interchangeably to the UK, which includes Northern Ireland, and to Britain (and British), which strictly speaking excludes it.

It matters not for this purpose that the Council and the universities fell out over the prices at which universities said they would teach their undergraduates – although the episode illustrates yet again the perturbed environment for planning which left the universities feeling harassed and beleaguered. It does perhaps also make again the case for unwrapping and adopting a new paradigm. The statements were carefully crafted, fashioned and presented. They explain each institution's mission, purposes, strategies and intended means of working.

In this book I construct a set of questions from a lifelong learning perspective to interrogate these planning statements about what the universities think they are, where they seek to go, what resources they require and how they mean to deploy them. What is unsaid may be as revealing as the overt statement of purpose and plan, and an eye is kept out for this as well. How far and in what ways are the universities seeking to become lifelong learning centres, other than through distinct short course continuing education?

There are different traditions and generations of universities, and I adopt a generally acknowledged rough categorization to assist the process of analysis and story-telling. The Scottish, Northern Irish and Welsh institutions are obviously different in respect of an additional arrangement with a Government office, and in the Scottish case also in terms of relationship with the school system: access (at seventeen plus rather than eighteen plus) is more open and participation rates are much higher (McPherson 1990: 3).

Within England the ancient universities are normally placed in a class apart, although some Scottish universities are of similar age. There is a set of large nineteenth-century civic universities in major centres of industry and population. London with its constituent colleges is a case on its own. A more recent set of civic universities, mostly originating as university colleges, are often called the redbricks. Then there are the former colleges of advanced technology which acquired university status in the 1960s, when the very similar polytechnics were separated off by the binary line. A set of new greenfield or plate glass universities was founded at the same time. Also included are the London and Manchester Business Schools, and Goldsmiths' College, now part of the University of London, but not the private University of Buckingham, Cranfield Institute of Technology or the Open University (OU), another 1960s foundation with a distinct CE identity and mission quite outside the residential 'finishing school' tradition. There is a sense in which the existence of the OU has provided a rationale for other universities not becoming more open; some have on occasion, albeit *sotto voce*, said as much.

Change processes and resistance to change

Modern times arrived for British universities with the financial cuts of 1981, which were savage in the case of such universities as Salford and Aston. The pressure has been sustained through the following decade, and we can ask when we examine the planning statements for the 1990s whether fundamental change has resulted. The Government sought via the Jarratt Committee (Jarratt 1985) to make universities more managerial: to create tighter, faster, more efficient systems for taking decisions, monitoring results and acting to rectify deficiencies. They have been required to report on their responses to Jarratt, and on the extent to which proposed changes have been implemented. Planning statements to the UFC reflect this 'Jarratt factor'. Apart from changes to committees and decision-making, changes that is to the formal structure of the organization, universities are now required to allocate part of their academic payroll on a merit or incentive basis. Additional payments must be made to staff deemed particularly valuable, either because of their productivity or because of their scarce market-value. This became a condition of receiving additional funds to pay academic salaries. Another requirement is that all academic staff be appraised by means of schemes approved by the UFC.

Other efforts towards the same end of enhancing productivity and managerial efficiency are mediated through the two CVCP units: the SDTU for staff development; and the AAU mainly to monitor what universities are themselves doing to enhance and monitor the quality of their teaching. Further change will in due course follow implementation of the 1991 HE White Paper (Clarke *et al.* 1991). Similarly, research is appraised by a UGC, now UFC, system, which has, predictably, been accused in turn of subjectivity, high cost and inefficiency. The funding of research is being separated increasingly from that of teaching – a further measure to monitor performance and exercise control.

There are two assumptions behind all this: that universities are inefficient; and that their efficiency will be improved by a series of external interventions, implemented largely top-down, and drawn in the main from the management practices and reward systems of other kinds of organizations. This is not a peculiarly British preoccupation. A comparative study of quality and access in higher education draws out parallels on each side of the Atlantic (Berdahl *et al.* 1991), and the following continental perspective also reveals similarities:

> European universities are currently searching for new management models. On the one hand, there is widespread criticism that the traditional managerial modes of a relatively weak rector, a limited number of administrative staff and a strong academic staff in decision-making at universities is no longer appropriate in time of increased importance of institutional policies. On the other hand, the U.S. model of institutional management is frequently criticised for subordinating academics and their rationale to a managerial class claiming to adhere to academic values, but in practice pursuing abstract managerial goals such as institutional growth and power.
>
> Teichler 1990: 12

Allen (1988: Chapter 3) echoes a view among organization theorists that universities are a unique form of organization because of their multiplicity of missions and the absence of a single absolute authority. They are a genus apart, a non-organization, or an organized anarchy, characterized by ambiguity, but not therefore 'illegitimate, immoral or ineffective' (Allen 1988: 26). More positively, the importance of organizational culture, tradition, intuition and above all motivation which characterizes universities as social systems may prove increasingly relevant to other knowledge-based industries, and indeed to all forms of industry, as 'human resources', human skill, ingenuity and motivation to do well become increasingly crucial – and as Fordist production line modes of supervision and quality control prove as ineffectual in other industries as they tend to be in the education and knowledge-production industry of higher education. The managerialist tide is still flowing strongly. Even staunch defenders of academic tradition concede that not all is well in the management and leadership of universities. At the same time there is increasing recognition that the more collegial traditions of universities, with stress upon individual and small group motivation, may have much to offer to other 'environment-serving' organizations like hospitals, and indeed to modern organizations more generally.

This affords a useful context for examining how the contemporary university presents itself and its planning. What mix do we find between: a complete shift towards managerialism; modest but real changes to streamline decision-making; token changes to satisfy the letter of Jarratt and get money from the UFC; or confident assertion that essentially the university is run on the right lines already? These are important questions for the university of the 1990s as pressure increases to sharpen its identity, in the process of clarifying goals and making choices over priorities. They are especially acute in the area of CE. Historically this has been left to the specialized, extramural and now continuing education, departments; and to such other departments and individuals as have been moved by community or entrepreneurial instincts.

The changed environment (UFC and wider) and the demand for more managerialism may be combining to centralize the development and management of CE in the UFC era. This happened in the United States at an earlier time. Extension became too important to leave to the extension people (witness Rockhill's 1983 history of university extension in California). It is a common refrain among CE folk in British universities that commitment and support from the top are crucial. This is balanced, however, by fear that 'mainstreaming' adult continuing education within the university may destroy its distinctive contribution; and in a more positive sense by recognition that persuasion rather than dictation may be necessary, if good university CE is to take place.

The culture of the university is an important factor, whether an aid or a hindrance, in doing more and better continuing education. It cannot be made simply by the vice-chancellor writing memoranda, or senate passing resolutions (see Palfreyman 1989; Duke 1989b; Fulton and Ellwood 1989; Reid 1990). The middle band of management in organizations is notoriously resistant to change that may prove more acceptable above and below. In universities this is the chairperson or head of department, flanked for instance by the admissions tutor. There may also be a powerful informal band of resistance, or alternatively of positive energy, in the form of 'the men in grey suits'. These may be long-standing senior lecturers (and usually they *are* men), not very visible in the formal hierarchy, yet wielding great influence, sometimes through committees but perhaps less formally, as the keepers of the university's identity – its essential, distinctive character.

Change, be it for CE, Access, 'enterprise', modularization or merger, may require a real push from the world outside; and a top-down and bottom-up 'pincer movement'; and some stick and some carrot; but also insinuation into the shadowy cultural heartland of the institution wherein change is supported, prevented or subverted. The formal arrangements within the formal structure for CE, even the formal reward systems to individuals and departments, will go only part of the way towards making universities centres of lifelong learning, if the men in grey suits would have it otherwise. We will do well to bear this in mind, in examining what universities *say* they mean to do, and to become, in the years ahead.

2 | Change and Higher Education – the New Discourse

Language in crisis

Much used of universities in recent years is the term *crisis*. It gave the title to a book by the Editor of *THES* (Scott 1984), and continues to feature in *THES* leaders and more recent books (see Duke 1990 for a review of such literature). The very use of the term becomes a factor in the situation, an influence on those managing, entering and leaving higher education. The *THES* main leader for 11 January 1991 asserted that

> there can be little doubt about the deepening crisis in universities ... its urgency is now palpable. There is a real risk that during the 1990s the self-confidence of the universities will collapse and their academic excellence will be in peril.

How deep is the change, and how valid the use of the term crisis?

Some insight can be gained into the direction, nature and rate of change by looking at the changing terminology used in and about HE. Is this new discourse a pointer to a new paradigm, quickly shaping if not yet fully formed? Who uses it? How freely, or with what discomfort and reluctance? The old-style department chairman in a recent popular and duly tele-dramatized satire of universities sought to mask his ignorance of 'viring' – a term found only in the Addenda to my *Shorter Oxford English Dictionary*. When the Training Agency's first, rather clumsy, document proposing 'enterprise' got around to universities some academic boards had schoolboy fun with its language. A year or two later universities jostled polytechnics to be in on the next funding tranche – another term newly insinuated into the discourse. So the word 'enterprise' has arrived – albeit often disguised as *EHE* – acronymania being itself a feature of the new modernity.

Not long ago I was mocked for using the term 'proact' – and the more pleased, therefore, to hear it used soon after at university senate by my (American-born) vice-chancellor. Polytechnics tend to use a more managerial language than universities: in advertising for senior appointments they offer private sector style 'packages'. Contrast Cambridge professors' public

Table 2.1 Terms of the 'new discourse'

General area	Old discourse	New discourse
Admissions	selection students A levels	Access, APEL clienteles, marketing non-traditional entry
Curriculum	subjects courses progression	core, options, modules capability, competence enterprise transferability, CAT
Learning–teaching processes	lectures seminars tutorials	negotiation experiential self-directed
Management and resources	collegiality community discourse grants investments fees	mission, system outputs appraisal, audit decisions, control business plans cash flow, cost centres bid prices, contracts student loans realization of assets partnership, PR franchising, validation
Measures, outcomes and results	educated class of degree drop-out/wastage academic standing	employable credits accumulated efficiency, PIs and PMs profiles, ROAs
Values and purposes	culture discipline excellence scholarship standards	efficiency fitness for purpose quality value added lifelong learning

refusal to accept differential remuneration, when the Government introduced and insisted upon differentiality.

Which are the newer terms now in use (or older terms used differently) in higher education? What does this suggest about institutions' response to new thinking, new fashions, new opportunities and new perturbation? One crude tabulation is given in Table 2.1.

Different attitudes to change

Table 2.1 illustrates a shift in vocabulary, especially towards the end of the 1980s. Much of the new language has invaded the universities from the worlds of government and business. The invasion has been more rapid and complete in other parts of FHE, for two obvious reasons.

First, the public sector lacked the relative autonomy enjoyed by universities under their charters. Indeed FE still comes under the local authorities, although its movement in the direction already taken by the polytechnics and colleges of higher education in 1989 is foreshadowed in the Further Education White Paper, which will have FE removed from local authority control with the creation of Further Education Funding Councils (DES 1991). These institutions have been less insulated against externally imposed change. As we shall see below, many of the attempted changes represented by this new terminology can be traced to one or another governmental body, quango or surrogate change agent; that is, to different players in the new environment of HE sketched in Chapter 1.

The second reason is that universities historically enjoy prestige and exclusive access to certain resources, including still in 1991 the use of the very term university and until recently the title of professor. This advantage has given them a stranglehold on traditional purposes and values – culture, discipline, excellence, scholarship, standards – and on funds for curiosity-driven research.

Polytechnics, particularly, have aspired to the same identity and resources that universities have traditionally monopolized. In rather conservative British society they have little chance of beating the universities at their own traditional game. On the one hand, therefore, the polytechnics have sought – successfully in the light of the Higher Education White Paper (Clarke *et al.* 1991) – to break into the exclusive use of the high-prestige term 'university', which gives a powerful market advantage in the competition for students, research contracts, charitable benefactions and so on. In 1989 they began to use the title professor. At the same time they are naturally more amenable to some re-definition of the purposes of higher education, as reflected in the newer language of discourse. This should help to level the playing field, and perhaps also shift the goalposts, reducing their relative disadvantage.

Continuing education and the new discourse

University continuing educators assert their academic bona fides and scholarly responsibilities as firmly as anyone – more stridently perhaps than colleagues in more established and prestigious fields. But their primary mission is quite clearly in the area of teaching. It is an anomaly, and probably a temporary one at that, that the funding of one kind of teaching in universities (of those working towards degrees) is defined and funded in one UFC compartment, whereas another kind of teaching (CE), which is becoming increasing indistinguishable as students mingle in the classroom and modular programmes become commoner, is funded separately. EMD and CE folk are, moreover, dedicated primarily, though not exclusively, to the teaching of adult and so by definition 'non-traditional' students.

It is therefore all but inevitable that CE serves at least as a conduit for the entry of new ideas and new language into the teaching life of the university. Sometimes this works in parallel, though only by accident, with the pressures for new discourse from outside. It is little wonder if EMD and CE personnel are looked at askance by those more traditional faculty members for whom change feels too rapid and innovation seems mostly to mean dilution, both of standards and of working conditions. Do extramuralists coming in out of the cold look like a Trojan horse to threaten the very citadel of the academy?

Much of the new language has found its way into the upper reaches of most universities, where it is mostly well understood. Judgements are made, based in reason and with calculation of institutional interest, as to how much to take on board how quickly. Universities' bids to the UFC reflect this. On the other hand, universities being the relatively anarchic non-organizations that they mostly still are, it is certain that many of the newer terms and ideas considered in this chapter are quite alien to the majority of university scholars: not so much that they are rejected, rather that they are 'nothing to do with us'. There is a problem, then, about knowing how far the changes apparently accepted by each university in formulating a planning statement and making offers to the UFC will take root, be implemented and become part of a changed culture for each institution. If the new discourse does represent a new paradigm, is this for real? Or is it merely skin-deep? Does it penetrate beyond the registrarial level of top management where responsibility for relating to the outside world, and for extracting the necessary resources, may be seen, however unwisely, still almost exclusively to reside?

Agencies of change

Which innovations are sought? What shifts in teaching activity, purpose and priority do they represent? Taken together they may justify use of the expression 'paradigm shift'. Note also who outside HE is championing the changes, and pressing them upon higher education, with what degree of success.

One naturally first considers the Department of Education and Science (DES) working to the Secretary of State for Education, with a junior minister for higher education. The Universities Funding Council (UFC) is technically quite separate from the DES, but it is not always clear how independently it acts. In Australia the analogous HE body (CTEC) has been replaced by an advisory committee within the Department of Employment, Education and Training (DEET), so at least things are more transparent. Possibly any gain in universities' arms-length relationship with government is outweighed by the loss in direct, undisguised governmental responsibility, and accountability, for policy; the new Australian situation might actually be better. On this basis the UFC and PCFC would not be merely merged (Clarke *et al.* 1991) but also absorbed into the DES, or into a combined Department of Employment, Education and Training.

The aims of the UFC (1989a) certainly, and naturally, reflect Government policy for the universities. The DES, and perhaps also the UFC as the agency mediating policy along with funds to the universities, tends to express the will of the Cabinet and Treasury to contain public expenditure, demanding economy and efficiency – more output at reduced per capita cost. Theirs is the language of performance indicators and performance measures (PIs and PMs); of accountability, cost reduction, staff appraisal and productivity payments. This appears to be the main source of the new managerial language invading HE, which is more disliked in the university than in the public sector of FHE.

The CVCP is another kind of mediating agency between government and individual universities, and is drawn into all of the issues which this book is about. Its role can be ambiguous and conflictual: reassuring government that efficiency and productivity are high and increasing; conveying to the general public and the press how valuable – and in the positive sense precious – the universities are; chivvying the membership to go along, to bend, far enough with government to avoid more destructive intervention in institutional, managerial or academic freedom. The CVCP's role in management and development is expressed through papers and press releases to its members and the wider world; and now also via the Staff Development and Training and Academic Audit Units (SDTU and AAU). Both units address the contemporary preoccupation with quality. They seek to enhance staff development, and to see that universities have, and fully use, good quality assurance mechanisms for their teaching.

The DES, and in its wake the UFC and CVCP, does of course go beyond accountancy and management, to policy and purpose. Kenneth Baker, as Secretary of State, made a policy commitment greatly to expand HE student numbers at a conference at Lancaster in January 1989, a commitment echoed by his successors. It implied a paradigm shift from the elite British to a mass HE system, widening access for both young and older 'non-traditional' (and so in the broad sense CE) students.

In CE, more narrowly understood, the DES has built up a substantial unit for Professional, Industrial and Commercial Updating (PICKUP), now led by a Head of Adult Vocational Education and Training. PICKUP funds, initially direct from the DES but subsequently, in the case of universities, via the UGC and now the UFC, are used to start up (or pump-prime) new vocational continuing education. The carrot is not large, but it is said to have moved the donkey a long way forward (DES 1989).

As we move more into the professional areas of teaching and learning the influence of other bodies, governmental and other, becomes more evident. We have seen that the DES, UFC and CVCP all play a role in influencing the shape and work of universities. Each has a different position in a governmental–NGO spectrum, and the role of each is in some sense ambiguous. Educational and professional issues entangle with the managerial and political. Staying with access for a moment, we find other players, with different identities again. Each of these players (or environmental influences) also has its own agenda, its own issues of identity and even survival. The space for ambiguity and for shifting positions and alliances is large indeed. Whether moving to a new paradigm or staying with the old one, institutional leaders must be sure and quick of foot.

The Council for National Academic Awards (CNAA) provides a good example of this. Its own *raison d'être* came under question when the PCFC sector left local authority control. Following the Bird Report in 1990 the CNAA's future remained uncertain well into 1991 (Bird and Callaghan 1990), when the Higher Education White Paper (Clarke *et al.* 1991) spelt out its demise. CNAA became an important access player by virtue of managing the Access Courses Recognition Group (ACRG), strictly a joint CNAA/ CVCP venture. This assumed responsibility for the quality control of access courses nationally. It tries to combine assurance on standards through a national network of Authorised Validating Agencies (AVAs) with 'lightness of touch' intended to foster diversity and to develop new forms of access. ACRG is transbinary. Its influence is just as powerful in universities as in polytechnics, and in the FE colleges which are the main Access course providers. Incidentally, and cautiously, CNAA tries via the ACRG to foster partnership among FHE institutions – one of the keywords in education's 'new paradigm' lexicon.

CNAA's influence on access (spelt with a small 'a' to distinguish it from Access courses) and its efforts for transbinary and wider partnership are expressed in other ways. In particular the CNAA Credit Accumulation and Transfer Scheme (CATS) has become a byword and the main vehicle for CAT development. Here we are looking not just at access into, within and between FHE institutions, but also at recognition, transfer and trading with industry, via recognition for academic credit of workplace learning. Thus CNAA is promoting large 'A' Access via ACRG, small 'a' access via CATS, and partnership, covertly, through both.

APEL, the accreditation of prior experiential learning, refers to the recognition for academic credit of learning which has occurred outside formal education: whether at work, in the community or, in future, as current research and development reaches fruition, in the home. Here the active proponents are further out from government. APEL is a keen preoccupation of the Unit for the Development of Adult Continuing Education (UDACE), part of the non-governmental grouping of NIACE agencies which were being pulled apart by government at the beginning of the 1990s. It is also the central concern of Norman Evans's non-profit-making NGO, the Learning through Experience Trust (LET). It is championed by the Open College Federations, which are increasingly organizing into a national network.

Access and APEL have their most immediate relevance at the point of admissions policy and practice. There may be a large gap between an institution's admissions policy and the practices of its admissions tutors down at the department coalface (Fulton and Ellwood 1989; Kelly 1991). CAT more obviously relates to the concept, construction and reform of curricula within the institution. In practice the main emphasis is on CAT within rather than between institutions, at least in the early years. This may change, should competition for students become fiercer. CAT cannot proceed far until courses are modularized and given a credit-rating.

Credit-rating can be superficial, largely arithmetical. Modularization, however, quickly takes one into quite fundamental questions of curriculum design – and beyond these to clarifying and perhaps modifying assumptions about the nature, intentions and outcomes of a university education. Likewise, although Access and APEL can be addressed, superficially, as simple admissions matters, they quickly lead to more fundamental questions about who comes to university with what learning needs and resources; and what this means for curriculum design and for teaching–learning processes. That is to say, Access, APEL and CAT can all be taken up superficially and accommodated at first within the established HE paradigm. However, each soon raises fundamental questions and favours a new paradigm. It is far from clear how far all, or some, universities will adopt these new arrangements, and behind them a new 'idea of a university'; or whether, as many sceptics believe, they are just expedients, and only skin-deep.

Four keywords

I conclude this short discussion of new discourse by looking at four keywords, and the agencies, or external change agents, which are promoting them. The words are *enterprise, capability, competence* and *partnership*. The agencies particularly, though in no sense exclusively, identified with them are TEED, the RSA, NCVQ and, a different kind of body again, CIHE.

I concentrate mainly on enterprise, and the Enterprise in Higher Education (EHE) programme of TEED. Capability is identified especially with the RSA, a venerable and prestigious professional association; and competence with the NCVQ. However, both of these words feature in the objectives of EHE, as indeed does partnership, for the TA (TEED) plays a wide field in fostering innovation in higher education, as *Higher Education Developments. The Skills Link* demonstrates (TEED 1990). Partnership might be called the hallmark of the Council for Industry and Higher Education (CIHE), a new, intendedly short-lived, voluntary association of a few of the 'great and the good', quite unlike the RSA despite some similarity of aims. Here are four quite different kinds of change agents: each with its particular style, strength and limitations; each trying to shift the work and identity of the universities.

Enterprise

After a decade of 'privatise' the loosely associated term enterprise might be expected not to resonate well with HE, which finds progressive privatization problematic, although that word has not been widely used of HE in Britain as such (contrast Jones and Anwyl 1987). Yet over one hundred HEIs bid for Enterprise funds at the earliest opportunity. Launched by the Secretary of

State for Employment at the end of 1987, but developed and run by the Training Agency, the EHE initiative seeks 'to assist institutions of higher education [to] develop enterprising graduates in partnership with employers' through grants of up to a million pounds over five years. There were four universities among the first eleven successful bids, and more in subsequent rounds (Training Agency 1989).

The TA was sensitive to the matter of new discourse which this chapter is about:

> 'Enterprise' has become part of the discourse of the nineteen eighties and is the buzz word in a number of circles . . . . It has also entered the vocabulary of educationists especially in relation to the debates about the enhancement of the work-related curriculum and the preparation of young people for employment. The debate centres on what skills young people in the latter part of the twentieth century will need to take them through to their adult, working life [note, not 'through their'] and how these skills can best be imparted.
>
> Narrow discipline-based knowledge learned in the classroom, the lecture theatre or the laboratory can nowadays become out of date in a relatively short space of time. Learning how to learn rather than absorbing facts and learning how to apply a body of knowledge are increasingly being regarded as equally important as the knowledge itself. . . . Education is responding to the changes in the work environment and to the needs of business and industry by looking to, and in many cases encouraging, the teaching of flexible, transferable skills, 'active' learning and more widespread use of educational technology and practical project work.
>
> Training Agency 1989: 2, 3

The account refers to other 'central initiatives', such as PICKUP and the RSA's 'Education for Capability' campaign, as well as to 'spontaneous' individual initiatives to 'embed' (a much favoured buzz word) the concept and practice. But 'it is thought that the pace of embedding enterprise in the HE curriculum needs to be accelerated'. It was to this that EHE was directed, both into the curriculum and in the work of the institutions at large. The booklet goes on to refer to CIHE's partnership efforts, which seek versatile and adaptable students via 'key competencies of communication, problem solving, teamwork and leadership'. EHE also

> emphasises effective learning and the role of the students in directing their own education programme. It strongly supports a broadening of the learning environment and a move towards less passive teaching styles. It encourages the use of such approaches as negotiated contracts of learning and team-work as well as flexible forms of accreditation and qualification. In this respect, EHE institutions have been asked to consider the longer term implications of an enterprise programme on policies of admission, access and educational credit . . . . EHE is posit-

ively linked to plans that encourage a more flexible system of entry to higher education. A more 'open' system could allow the unemployed or non-traditional students and those in employment to benefit from higher education at various stages in their lives and not simply the narrow group who presently constitute the majority of undergraduates....

The intention is that enterprise programmes offer more than simple, bolt-on modules of business studies. [Bolt-on is another common buzz-word: the unacceptable opposite of embedding, be it of CE, Access or Enterprise.] There should be an attempt to integrate the new program-mes with the educational provision already offered to the students.

Training Agency 1989: 4, 5

The Training Agency could scarcely be more explicit about what it looks for through its million-pounds-per-institution intervention. Note the many 'new discourse' terms in these extracts; and the cumulative implication for shifting HE efforts (further) away from the older academic paradigm – although the TA also insisted that EHE was 'not a narrow vocational substitution for broad academic education and does not displace the need for high level expertise and professionalism in any number of specialisms' (Training Agency 1989: 5).

In 1991 it is too early to judge the ultimate impact of EHE, which is being monitored in various ways by TEED (TEED 1991). Rumour has it that some institutions have simply 'taken the money and run' – or, more accur-ately, renegotiated what they will actually do when they have won the contract and as movement begins. For some it is essentially a staff develop-ment project, this being, it is said, the key to institutional change. Un-doubtedly there will be some shifting of funds to other, albeit connected, purposes.

The important question is whether the less tangible but most central institutional change objectives will be tackled, or alternatively subverted. Another important point is the connectedness of the change programmes, slogans and initiatives which the extracts quoted above display, and their closeness to a shift towards what is required for recurrent education and lifelong learning. This does not feature directly at all. On the other hand a wider review of trends suggests that recurrent education has regained sup-port as a strategy for university reform in Europe more generally (Teichler 1990: 8).

Partnership

The Council for Industry and Higher Education symbolizes partnership through its small and exclusive membership of vice-chancellors and senior industrialists. It promotes it through its publications, which are few and brief but clear and, in a society still conscious of status and deferential to those who wield power, probably influential. In *Towards a Partnership* the Council states that

Government, higher education and industry need to become partners in developing a *different kind of higher education system* to provide for larger numbers, recruit them from a much wider segment of the population, and offer them a diversity of learning methods and opportunities, often work-related, at different stages of their lives. . . .

There are not yet real signs of the major change of emphasis in HE institutions towards continuing education and in particular towards professional updating and retraining. . . .

A whole-hearted marketing effort by institutions is needed nationally but cannot be mustered while continuing education remains an under-funded, spare-time activity for most academic departments.

CIHE 1987: 1–2, original emphasis

The Council's approach is to encourage debate about the aims of higher education, and about the common interests and values of industrialists and, for example, those teaching the humanities:

the relevance of the humanities in higher education in the next century ought to be no more in question than it has ever been. The *criteria* of relevance, however, as seen both by professionals of the disciplines and by outsiders, deserve to be rethought, brought up to date, and restated.

CIHE 1990: 1

This report goes on to refer to capabilities, and to the general intellectual skills and particular personal qualities, along with demonstrated academic abilities, which employers most seek. Here the emphasis appears to be on re-thinking and re-stating, rather than on root and branch reform. Thus

students need to be taught by people who are fully confident of the special values and educational power of what they do, and who are able to convince students of its worth to them . . . the most important function of higher education is to inspire its students with a passionate inquisitiveness to continue learning throughout life.

CIHE 1990: 2, 3

In a lecture at the University of Hull, Patrick Coldstream, Director of CIHE, called for the education of *adaptable* people:

what is *chosen* with the choice of first degree subjects are the *languages* – again I use the word broadly – which determine how the learner will grasp the world – the *language* in which she or he will ask questions about it.

Coldstream 1991: 2

We should ask ourselves: (a) whether education for capability in this sense is a matter of re-thinking and re-stating current practice – of learning and adopting a new vocabulary to explain existing good practice rather than actually changing the goals of a university education; and (b) whether a passion for lifelong learning is currently part of (perhaps unstated) object-ives, rather than a (threatening) new requirement to put upon teachers in

HE. Affirmative answers to both of these questions can still mean a new paradigm for higher education: for a paradigm is a way of seeing and understanding, a new way of recognizing what perhaps has already emerged unnoticed from the chrysalis. There may be a great deal in a name.

Capability

Capability, mentioned above, is also being promoted, especially by the RSA – the Royal Society for the Encouragement of Arts, Manufactures and Commerce, to give it its full name – which dates from the mid-eighteenth century and, like CIHE, may have acceptability that is denied to the DES and TEED by virtue of its prestigious professional standing. It enjoys sponsorship to conduct projects to do with higher education from a number of sources, including BP, which funded the RSA access initiative managed by Sir Christopher Ball.

Access is concerned with getting people into HE. The RSA's Higher Education for Capability project seeks to develop students' capacity to be lifelong learners and to cope with continuous change, once they are in. Key themes include building actively on students' interests and experiences before and after entry into HE, negotiation, active and interactive learning, and new forms of assessment calculated to enhance learners' responsibility and accountability.

While there is much in common with EHE there are also crucial differences. With more holistic emphasis on the development of the person, including building up people's confidence and competence through opportunities to take responsibility for their own learning and to relate it to their own development, and to the world around them. Stress is upon learning for life, of which paid work is but one part.

Most of the funding of the HE for Capability project comes from the TA, now TEED. Its concern was to provide a longer lasting vehicle than EHE could offer for raising the wider issues of change in HE, to do for instance with management, quality, employers and professional bodies, which flow from the more specific curricular changes brought about by individuals and course teams. It is no easy matter to ascertain how far projects and reports, and the related consultations and seminars, such as those of the RSA, have practical influence. Probably they help cumulatively to shift the grounds of discourse, insinuate and normalize new terminology, and so build up the pressure for 'flip-over' to a new paradigm (see, for example, RSA 1988; Ball 1989, 1990; Parry 1990).

Competence

Competence is an increasingly well-worked term. Enterprise is established (if not always welcomed by all) in the universities as well as in PCFC sector discourse. Capability is reasonably well known in the latter, and probably not unacceptable in universities either, if much less used there. Insofar as competence is identified with national vocational qualifications (NVQs), and equated with the work of the NCVQ, it is much less well known or understood. Insofar as it is understood in the NVQ sense, it is also less acceptable to universities.

The National Council for Vocational Qualifications (NCVQ) is charged with developing a simplified national system of vocational qualifications, thereby clearing the 'vocational qualifications jungle'. Confusion hampers access to higher education and employment alike. NVQs are conceived initially as being at four or five levels, the higher levels equating in level with the work of HE. The task of creating viable NVQs at the lower levels is proving substantial. The FE sector has already fully engaged with NVQs and is wrestling to secure future business by teaching to the NVQ system. The universities appear barely to have registered the existence of NCVQ, and the possible implications for their curricula.

A UDACE project on learning outcomes funded by the Employment Department explores ways of describing and assessing the outcomes of degree level study, focusing on five subject groups. The project's consultative document asks whether learning outcomes are the same as competences:

> There has recently been considerable debate about the meaning of competence and its place in Higher Education . . . . There are two major concerns in the academic world about the notion of competence. The first is a fear of vocationalism – that important dimensions of higher education which relate to the development of the person, to the acquisition and transmission of cultural and social values, may be lost. . . . The second is a fear of reductionism . . . .
>
> The project has found widespread ignorance, in higher education, of the role of the National Council for Vocational Qualifications . . . . Many of the HE staff consulted . . . expressed concern about the nature of developments in vocational education. Some clearly saw it as a threat to academic standards and autonomy but few had any real knowledge of the principles or the practices of standards development . . . . The project subject groups have tended to avoid the use of competences in the development of learning outcomes.
>
> UDACE 1991: 5–6

It cannot, however, be long before the work of NCVQ is felt in higher education, as some professions put their preparation on to the competency basis required to win it NCVQ rating. Competences, NCVQ style, can be seen positively as requiring clarity, and clear communication, about teaching objectives and learning outcomes – and so perhaps as little different from CIHE's call for re-statement and renewed confidence in teaching the humanities. Or they can be seen as mechanistic – concentrating on the measurable and skill-based, to the exclusion of the more complex and less tangible learning outcomes which, in old-style parlance, create the 'educated man', and the truly competent professional.

In summary, a stream of new terms, or more accurately of well-known terms carrying new and particular meanings, is now entering the discourse of higher education. Most are carriers, and also surrogates, for an outside initiative to change, or accelerate change in, the curriculum of HE. Some come with a dowry, small like PICKUP, larger like Enterprise, or non-specific but potentially much larger still, like (industrial) partnership. Most also carry a price tag. Sometimes this is writ deceptively small. The hidden cost in time, and the partly hidden implication of effort for institutional change, may be substantial. The same applies to another nineties buzzword, quality, which is considered in Chapter 6.

Do these terms, some or all of them, also imply a sell-out of what is valuable, unique, in the university tradition? Does the picture thrown up by projecting on to the screen this 'new discourse' justify the term crisis in higher education? Is it witness to that crisis, or stepping stones, rather, to new and firmer ground for university education? If a new paradigm is emerging, how soon and how surely will universities recognize and adopt it? In the chapters that follow, we will test some of these propositions and answer some of these questions.

3 | Mission, Aims and Objectives – What May Be New?

Purpose in higher education

> There is a particular crisis facing higher education which has been largely overlooked. It is a crisis to do with the way in which we understand higher education, the fundamental principles on which the idea of higher education has traditionally stood, and the way in which those principles are being undermined.
>
> Barnett 1990: 3

Barnett sees this undermining as both epistemological and sociological. He uncovers the 'contested' nature of the HE concept, referring in turn to the Greek, to the medieval and Newman's ideas, then to Karl Jaspers, and later to the counter course conception of HE of the late 1960s. Has the idea of higher education now disappeared?

> The concept of the 'multiversity' is testimony to the increasing incoherence of institutions of higher education: with their competing missions of service, scholarship, military and commercial research, access, and income generation, they have no single sense of direction.
>
> Barnett 1990: 26

In concluding, Barnett takes up the theme of

> the fragmentation of the academic community into continually proliferating sub-communities. The development is so entrenched and so pervasive in its effects that it is misleading to talk of a single academic community.
>
> Barnett 1990: 201

This echoes the consideration in Chapter 1 of the nature of universities as organizations. Yet Barnett (1990: 8–9) does identify a common value background of higher education along these lines:

1. The pursuit of truth and objective knowledge.
2. Research.
3. Liberal education.

4. Institutional autonomy.
5. Academic freedom.
6. A neutral and open forum for debate.
7. Rationality.
8. The development of the student's critical abilities.
9. The development of the student's autonomy.
10. The student's character formation.
11. Providing a critical centre within society.
12. Preserving society's intellectual culture.

We may scan this list in vain for explicit reference to lifelong learning. Items 8 and 9 are compatible with a lifelong learning perspective. Item 10 smacks rather of pre-mature socialization. Items 6 and 11 sit comfortably with a traditional adult education value for universities, which is perhaps itself uncomfortable while HE is monitored with so critically political an eye – Barnett writes of witchcraft, but not of witch-hunts! Another contemporary analyst suggests that 'there is, or should be, something about higher education (or perhaps the highest education) which is peculiarly adult' (Tight 1991: 112).

Barnett disputes the functionalism or instrumentalism that prevails in public debates about higher education:

[The functionalist view] includes the tendency to understand higher education in terms of the values and goals of the wider society, and the drive to evaluate the effectiveness of higher education in terms of its demonstrable impact on the wealth-generating capacity of society. As a result, the costs of higher education and its contribution to the economy through supplying qualified personnel come to the fore ... issues of this type exercise a disproportionate influence in two senses. First, even as reflecting the interests of the wider society, they reflect a narrow set of interests .... Secondly, and more significantly, the functionalist approach neglects the *intrinsic* character of higher education.

Barnett 1990: 4–5

The subject matter of this book undoubtedly leans in the instrumental direction. We are about to see what the UFC sought of universities by way of planning statements, and what it received. Planning and bidding to such a prescription must be instrumental. Notions of lifelong learning, of preparing citizens for the 'learning society', also incline in this direction; there is no necessary discord with Barnett's twelve shared values. Indeed, extramural departments have tended to champion the liberal cause more boldly than their parent institutions.

Writing about part-time higher education, Malcolm Tight notes the paucity of discussion of purpose in British higher education, including the barrenness of official pronouncements, from the Robbins Report of 1963 to the late 1980s. He draws from international studies as well as UK practice five main purposes: skills development; selection; socialization; scholarship; service; adding, with similar alliteration, the possibly cynical sixth, self-perpetuation

or, simply, survival (Tight 1991: 119–22). To these we might add the
cultural transmission which was the fourth Robbins function: 'transmission
of a common culture and common standards of citizenship' (Committee on
Higher Education 1963: 7). Note the connection with a point which Barnett
makes after commenting on fragmentation of the academic community: that
this increasing differentiation is part of the 'wider fragmentation of the
culture of modern society' (Barnett 1990: 201).

Aims, resources and the UFC

I turn from this preliminary consideration of current, generally instrumental,
approaches to purpose in higher education, for which I am indebted to
Ronald Barnett's recent work, to the aims of British universities in the 1990s,
and the place of continuing education (for lifelong learning) in these. The
tension between essential, or liberal, higher education and instrumental,
functional, mostly employment-oriented education which Barnett, Silver and
Brennan and others consider will inevitably surface from time to time as we
examine universities' planning statements, and especially the place in these
of plans for CE. CE echoes and magnifies seemingly timeless debates about
the aims and purity of education.

The new funding and contracting era in British higher education was
heralded in the White Paper *Higher Education: Meeting the Challenge*, and
elaborated in a DES note on contracts (DES 1987). This sought to explain
what the replacement of grants by a system of contracting with the UFC's
successor would mean. The expected advantages were summarized (DES
1987: 4–5) as

(a) a greater precision in the specification of what is expected of institutions
    in return for public funding; leading to
(b) closer links between funding and institutions' performance in delivering
    specified provision; backed up by
(c) periodic re-negotiation of contracts taking account of institutions' relat-
    ive performance.

The paper suggested that this merely formalized what was implicit in earlier
funding arrangements. Universities gained little sense of what they might
expect of the UFC until they received its Aims in July 1989 and the main
letter about funding and planning, known as Circular letter 39/89, in that
December (UFC 1989a, b). Before then Circular letter 15/89 had invited CE
bids for 1990–1 from all universities (closing date 15 November 1989). Thus
CE gave universities some foretaste of bidding to and hearing from the UFC
before the main integrated bid for 1991–2 to 1994–5 went in, in June 1990.
The CE results for the first year were announced in March 1990.

The DES 1987 note reeked of the managerialism and a little of the new
discourse described in Chapter 2. More illuminating are the Aims which the
UFC issued following consultation with universities, and which begin with
this general aim:

The maintenance and development of universities as high-quality and cost-effective institutions, providing for the advancement of knowledge, the pursuit of scholarship and the education of students, thereby playing their part in meeting national needs.

The words quality and cost-effective are followed in the next aim by full accountability as a framework for autonomy, then there is an aim of increasing the range of choice in the university sector 'for organisations and for others seeking its services', as well as for students. For students, and with strong support reported for specific reference to both CE and a wider social mix, the aims are:

A growing range of opportunities for initial and continuing education to be offered to both full-time and part-time students and to both young and mature students.

The range of social and educational backgrounds of students to be broadened and the participation of under-represented groups to be increased.

The Aims make reference: to general accessibility of the fruits of scholarship and research 'to external organizations and individuals, in both the private and public sectors'; to the expansion of the roles of universities to make 'an increasing contribution to other areas of society (e.g. industry, commerce, the public service)' (contrast Barnett's concern over a superfluity of roles already!); to an expanding role 'in regional and local life as widely-recognised resource and advice centres which are readily accessible to appropriate institutions, organisations and individuals'; and to increasing collaboration with other further as well as higher education institutions – FE being added specifically in respect of access courses (UFC 1989a).

These Aims reappeared as Annon B to the UFC's main letter (39/89), which set out how the Council sought to realize them in the coming four-year period. Universities were to submit planning statements along with offers of student places and a portfolio of CE provision. Since research was being handled separately, using information already held from the research 'selectivity exercise', the focus was on teaching: principally in the mainstream, and secondarily in CE, now integrated with the main bid but as a separate portfolio. The letter referred to good quality and responsive educational services from 'a more market-oriented system in which market forces generated by institutional initiative and student choice are given greater play'. A substantial increase in numbers in higher education was sought through competitive bidding. The particular aim in respect of continuing education was 'to promote its development as an integral part of university activity, to encourage innovation and to rationalise funding'. Here as so often we see aims drifting into a prescription about means as well as economy.

Within this framework the UFC offered guidance on the preparation of planning statements. These were not just to show how each university proposed to develop its activities, and what specific objectives it was setting itself, but what contribution each university plans to make towards achieving the Council's Aims, and whether its plans include innovative proposals in areas of interest to the Council, notably more intensive use of accommodation and facilities, and facilitating or encouraging access to university education by other than qualified school leavers.

UFC 1989b: 8

Annex C to the letter (immediately following the UFC Aims as Annex B) explained that

the planning statement should be derived from the University's regular planning processes, and should reflect the results of the University's asking itself what sort of institution it wishes to be in the long term and what steps are necessary to achieve this.

More specifically the UFC looked to each university for ('described precisely'):

- its distinctive position within higher education and society as a whole
- any long-term aims or aspirations and strategies to achieve them

as well as for specific objectives and timings for the immediate four-year period. Universities were told to have in mind(!):

- Government policies and the Council's Aims set out in Circular letter 19/89
- relevant changes in society, especially scientific and technological change
- demographic factors, the demand from applicants and the demand or need for graduates
- relations with schools and the further education sector
- collaboration with other higher education institutions
- local, regional or international considerations
- the development of cooperation with industry and commerce.

The Council was nothing if not thorough in setting out the rules for this important examination paper. Subsequent paragraphs provided guidance for sections on academic shape (including 'characteristics which differentiate the University's academic programme from those elsewhere' – note the British preoccupation with institutional uniqueness); academic units and academic services; teaching and learning; student recruitment; research ('this section is included because there are indissoluble links between a teaching strategy and a research strategy'); continuing education; and finally budgetary policy and projected financial position.

The checklist on teaching and learning went beyond general policy, standards and quality, and perhaps staff development and appraisal, to require the following:

- curriculum policy, including the university's response to developments in secondary education, to the need to increase student access and to calls for courses with industrial or commercial components
- major curriculum changes and any associated resource implications

- developments for modular courses and arrangements for credit transfer
- the balance of provision for full-time and part-time study
- teaching methods, the use of new technology and any associated resource implications
- student assessment and examinations
- welfare and counselling services as academic support services
- any staff recruitment or retention problems which affect the provision of teaching.

For continuing education, which was covered more fully in separate advice, the general letter suggested 'strategy, objectives and priorities specific to continuing education although the relationship with the University's other academic activities should also be made clear'. The section might refer to some of the following:

- planned major changes in organizational arrangements, especially for former 'responsible body' work
- demand, including related market research
- the range, balance and mode of provision
- teaching arrangements, the extent of integration with other academic activities and any quality control mechanisms specific to continuing education
- student assessment and certification
- funding arrangements, including income generation.

Despite Government rhetoric about autonomous institutional enterprise, these notes of guidance show how closely the framework was prescribed by the UFC. With regard to language, strictly these are not *bids for funds*, much less *applications for grants*. Instead they are *offers* which may become the basis of *contracts*. In these circumstances, and with the UFC Aims so firmly written in and included as an annexe to the main letter, universities would deviate in the ways in which they expressed institutional uniqueness only at their peril. Circular 39/89 on Funding and Planning is a quite prescriptive and directive requirement for universities to plan to order, and to produce this plan as the basis for securing what was previously thought of as the core block grant funding on which they essentially depended.

This is the background to understanding the instinct of some vice-chancellors to free universities from reliance on government funding. There is still the possibility that some specialized institutions or parts thereof, perhaps selected business schools, might seek to go private, re-asserting autonomy as chartered foundations. The route, however, is hazardous. Most HEIs will continue to rely on students having the means, presumably mainly from government by some mix of fees, loans or vouchers, to pay the full cost of a university education. The contradiction between free market theory and centralized directive practice is likely to persist. We can sidestep this fraught area in this book, simply noting that in one way or another government will have to go on paying a large part of the cost if higher education is to expand as government has prescribed.

The diversity of universities

We might feel sure that each university would anyway emphasize to the UFC how it is special and different, the inclination exaggerated by the opening UFC injunction 'to describe concisely its distinctive position within higher education and society as a whole'. Keep this in mind through the succeeding chapters. The invitation to make offers was an invitation that could not realistically be refused. Given universities' organizational characteristics and the context of the bidding exercise, how literally can planning statements be taken?

An allied question is how different it is possible for universities to be within the one political and cultural context. Only one university digressed from the spirit of the letter to the point of starting by saying in so many words that it aimed to do and be what all universities do and are. Among the sixty-six statements and offers there were obvious patterns and resonances. Do these correspond with the categories identified in Chapter 1, and do they range in any tidy way along a conservative–innovative or an old–new paradigm spectrum? The short answer is that they do not. In the rest of this chapter I examine how the different universities and university colleges presented themselves; gain some sense of why this might be; and create a framework for more detailed consideration of issues related to continuing education and lifelong learning in later chapters.

The groupings are not clear-cut. Oxford and Cambridge are a class on their own, but there are very old universities in Scotland, where Aberdeen is approaching its 400th anniversary, an event Glasgow has passed. Edinburgh is of similar antiquity. The Scottish universities are distinct by virtue of their relationship with the Scottish Education Department and the school system, although there is diversity within this club of eight. They have three-year ordinary and four-year honours degrees; and there is a stronger tradition of attending the local university. Heriot-Watt is technological, a former college of advanced technology. Strathclyde, with eighteenth-century origins, also has a strong technological orientation, while Stirling is a new foundation. UCACE recognizes a distinct Scottish grouping. Closer European links have strengthened a Scottish sense of distinctness, and of alternative futures beyond those promised from London. Indeed, the 'European factor' is evident in many of the statements, and from two distinct angles: those distant from London who see prospects of a new Euro-centred regionalism; and others, mainly close to the Continent, for whom easy communications to Europe promise new business prospects.

The six Welsh colleges are, similarly, a distinct group in respect of relating to a Principality administration; yet they are diverse in size, history, breadth or specialism, with the University of Wales College of Medicine at one extreme. Cardiff (UWC Cardiff strictly), was created in 1988 from a merger of UCC and UWIST, following a crisis which threatened closure of a major UK university institution. It resembles in some respects one of the two Northern Ireland universities, Ulster, created earlier in the decade from the

UK's only full transbinary merger: between the New University of Ulster (NUU) and Ulster Polytechnic.

Ulster and the older Queen's University Belfast differ from other UK universities in their governmental relationships as well as in their fractured community setting. Their statements reflect particular sensitivity to the needs of the community, and the context of community division in which they exist. Ulster is unique in respect of the diversity of its levels of work – an inheritance from the polytechnic, which at least in terms of size 'took over' NUU. Whereas UWIST merged with UCC, the University of Manchester Institute of Science and Technology (UMIST) retains its distinct identity. Other highly specialized free-standing institutions are the London and Manchester Business Schools (LBS and MBS).

London University is unique, a category on its own. Fourteen constituent colleges furnished the UFC with separate statements and offers. Some are large and highly prestigious, like Imperial and University Colleges, some also highly specialized – for pharmacy, agriculture, law, and Oriental and African languages. Specialized as some are, the question still arises whether each sees a role for itself as a lifelong learning centre in its own professional area. Quite different are Birkbeck and now (since it recently joined London University) Goldsmiths', with their exclusive or strong orientation to part-time and adult study. Birkbeck, like the OU, is in the broader sense entirely a CE institution. However, its main funding is for part-time degrees, and so not for CE work as administratively defined, although it also has a substantial CE programme and UFC allocation.

Taking out Northern Ireland, Scotland, Wales, London, the OU and the two specialized business schools, it is easier, if still superficial, to group the English universities: ancient; generally large nineteenth-century civic; newer redbrick foundations often starting life as university colleges; the 1960s technological universities, formerly colleges of advanced technology; and the new greenfield or plate glass universities also of the 1960s.

History is important. It is significant for institutional culture. It affects the kinds of resources institutions enjoy, or lack; the kinds of structures by which they organize themselves and do their work; and the reigning assumptions about the nature of a university and of a university education from which they must continue to build, or, as it may be, to move away. Thus Scottish universities have been apprehensive that Scottish Highers and the general degree may disappear beneath a kind of English imperialism. Meanwhile some English universities are loosening the shackles of the three-year honours degree through modularization and interdisciplinarity, and there is talk, albeit perhaps more in the public sector, about developing intensive two-year degrees (see, for instance, Wagner in the *Guardian* of 9 April 1991).

On the other hand, some universities which had largely abandoned their local identity as civic foundations are putting down local roots again. National and international reputation may not be enough to win the resources needed from central government. The local 'commmunity', in at least some senses, again looks important. Manchester recalls its Owen's College origins;

the names of Joseph Chamberlain and Jesse Boot are intoned again in Birmingham and Nottingham; and youthful Warwick, calumnied for supping with industry in the early 1970s, adds other local benefactors to the early name of Rootes.

Summing up, there are indeed broad categories or families of universities, grouped according to their history, size, location and consequent similarities of structure and style. To the visitor from California, home of two insightful commentators on the HE scene, Milton Stern and Martin Trow, they all look rather similar, and rather like the polytechnics, compared with university or HE systems in North America, Europe and elsewhere.

I will keep this perspective periodically in sight. For the moment, however, let us concentrate on the diversity of universities: that distinctiveness which the UFC asked each to spell out. From this, and with an eye especially to CE within the larger picture, we can get to grips with the processes of and resistances to change, and get clearer not just whether but also how a new paradigm for universities in Britain might emerge.

Continuing education in the aims and objectives

Universities' interest in addressing the UFC was in making a case for increased student numbers at an acceptable price. 'Statements of the nature of the university: its aims and objectives', sought to establish this (the UFC's Aims implied increased numbers at reduced cost without loss of quality). Each university played to its distinctive strength within the rules and using the hints given by the Council. For some this meant building continuing education centrally into their aims and objectives, perhaps portraying them- selves as community-oriented universities. Not too much should be made of particular points included in or left out of the statements. More powerful is the sense in some statements that the university does indeed stand on three legs of teaching, research and service; that there is purposiveness in striving for this balance. Where the term 'balance' was used, however, it was more usually about subject balance: policy preference for science and technology against market demand for social studies and humanities.

Most universities made a good fist of arguing for CE funds in that separate section of the planning statement specifically to do with CE. This section allowed bids for ongoing liberal adult education, for new developments in continuing vocational education and for CE research. Because our interest is in the central transformation of universities towards a lifelong learning model I largely ignore these bids for 'short course CE', even though, true to UFC coaching, many universities emphasized its 'mainstreaming'.

No university presented CE as in conflict with teaching or research in its aims and objectives. The preoccupation was, rather, with showing how to reconcile high and rising research standing with high standards of teaching for larger numbers of students. Some institutions saw their future viability in larger student numbers and economies of scale. Credibility in respect of CE may have been a means to this end rather than a central preoccupation. In a way this makes it easier to test the statements for evidence of 'new paradigm' thinking: energies and consciousness were focused elsewhere.

Explicit mention of CE in the aims and objectives may therefore signify less than the general tenor of the statements. Tension between different roles did not feature apropos CE in these opening paragraphs, which ran from barely a page up to five and even ten pages. There were, however, important clues as to whether espousal of CE went beyond tokenism. Some aims and objectives conveyed a clear sense of community service and involvement, expressed through a cluster of aspirations, such as local collaboration, the practical application as well as scholarly dissemination of research findings, access and flexibility of services and provision generally. At the other extreme, the only reference to CE in two instances was as one component of an income stream intended to balance the books.

More positively, some universities referred to increasing CE as part of an increase in total teaching effort. This is quite logical: CE is one form of teaching, alongside work with undergraduate and graduate students, and its future may lie in this direction rather than as a distinct 'third leg' of community service. A small number of aims and objectives made a different connection: between the university's special research strength and dissemination of this expertise via CE.

Can we connect the conventional groupings of universities explained above with the broad impression conveyed by the aims and objectives of each institutional response? What about the historic dichotomy between RB and non-RB universities which has been a source of tension and has at times threatened to split RB from non-RB departments?

History, academic standing and continuing education

On the face of it we might expect two things. First, ex-RB universities with their historic, sometimes very large, EMDs (now also ex- in terms of the names, as we saw in Chapter 1) might give CE a much higher profile in their aims and objectives than other universities. Secondly, given the traditional marginality of continuing education compared with research and undergraduate teaching, CE might be rather poorly represented among the aims and objectives of the strongest and most prestigious universities, and more salient in weaker institutions struggling for distinct identity and perhaps a unique, local niche. Local access and CE in the immediate catchment area lends itself to such a definition of mission. If there is no chance of beating the winners at their own game – the conventional criteria of top-grade research and eighteen plus recruitment – there is something to be said for creating and winning by some new rules, as Salford has done, or for revisiting some older rules or 'ideas of a university'.

There are significant relationships along these lines, but the situation is not as tidy as this would imply. It may be hazardous as well as impolitic to identify 'weaker institutions'. The UFC (as formerly the UGC) has its semi-public 'worry list' based on management and financial viability. Top of the list was UC Cardiff, now part of the merged Cardiff institution. Aberdeen and Hull have been marked out in the past. London and several of its constituent colleges are often mentioned. At the end of 1990 Bristol, Edinburgh and Liverpool appeared to nominate themselves. However, financial standing and academic stature are not the same thing. Most institutional managers recognize that, whatever its virtues, CE is not the most sensible way to seek substantial new net income and solve a financial crisis. Academic standing is the more relevant criterion. The recent Research Selectivity exercise gave a 'top ten' by average research ratings. Some obviously prestigious institutions are missing from this list but it matters little for the immediate purpose. Included were Cambridge, Oxford, Imperial, LSE, UCL, Warwick, Essex, Bristol, York and UMIST – but not, for instance, Birmingham, Edinburgh, Glasgow, Leeds, Manchester, Nottingham or Southampton. Each of these can lay claim to high international status, as indeed can most UK HEIs in one area or another.

Let us take these ten as academically outstanding, note which of the sixty-six institutions enjoyed RB status and exercise judgement as to which of their planning statements implied real commitment to CE, broadly or narrowly understood, in the aims and objectives where the competition for space in stating institutional mission was keen. The results are shown in Table 3.1 There is some correlation between traditional RB provision and making CE central to the nature of the university as sketched to the UFC, but far from complete coincidence. Ten ex-RB universities give only modest weight to CE in terms of the kind of universities they aspire to be. Seven ex-RBs virtually ignore it up front.

Table 3.1 does not support the view that CE is mainly for low-status universities. There is only one ex-RB among the seven high-scoring research institutions in the right-hand column – three are London colleges, and London's RB role was carried by the federal EMD, now part of Birkbeck. More diverse, institution-specific, reasons explain the high or low rating given by universities to CE and related community service roles. For some it has to do with their particular orientation and mix of work. Thus LBS is strictly an all-CE (all post-experience) institution, Bradford an ex-college of advanced technology with a strong record in CVE and a broad perception of what CE should embrace. Oxford has recently undertaken a major review of its CE role after over a century of service and evolution as a major extra-mural provider (Brundin 1990), and has resolved upon significant further development.

The reference point for several London colleges is international scholarship and world class status. London has a unique and complex structure, with LAE till recently delegated to the little-loved federal centre. Some of the colleges clearly belong within the established paradigm: competition between bright youngsters for places, high A level scores and international research standing, buttressed now by national research ratings. Other kinds of institutions also bunch around this identity. York, with a good research rating,

Table 3.1 Academic standing and commitment to CE in aims and objectives

	CE central to mission	*Standard CE reference*	*CE marginal or absent*
All statements	17	19	30
Top ten by research	2	1	7
Ex-RB institutions	9	10	7

lacks a natural and unserved hinterland for a major regional CE role. Several Welsh colleges perhaps take for granted a familiar extramural role but fail to see possibilities for making a wider sense of CE central to future identity.

On the other hand, some who are located at one end of the spectrum might, with a little re-interpretation, relocate at the other extreme. Several universities made little or no mention of CE, yet clearly have a sense of mission and even, like Salford, an explicit mission statement which makes them essentially community or service-oriented institutions. Not only is it surprising to find Salford thus (mis)locating itself. It is similarly striking that LBS and MBS appear as polar opposites – suggesting that we have not a linear continuum but something more like a loop, in which Salford and MBS meet 'round the back' with Bradford and Birkbeck, LBS and Aberdeen, Leicester and Warwick.

A few universities, Lancaster for example, thus prove hard to place. They say much about, for instance, Open College and access, flexibility and modularization, but do not mention CE as such. Others with strong historic strength in one or another form of CE are re-organizing their CE arrangements and leave a somewhat ambiguous message about the future. Central administration claims that they are on the road to mainstreaming CE. Some observers fear they are witnessing, rather, its dissolution. Evidently it *is* relevant to speak of paradigms and a paradigm shift, or its absence. Different universities tend to present similar phenomena in very different ways, according to their currently preferred paradigms.

So there are problems of interpretation, varieties of self-presentation and hedging of bets in a few cases where major change in CE coincides with bidding to the UFC. These exemplify rather than negate the value of interrogating statements of aims and objectives about a CE mission. In the sections of the bids explicitly to do with CE there is not the same internal competition for mission headlines. The information is more straightforward but also, in a mission sense, less revealing.

Universities and their communities

What about new discourse as a pointer to a new paradigm?

The term mission wins little favour. Some of the new curriculum terms do appear – competence at Cardiff, transferable skills at St David's (Lampeter) and, along with capability, Aberdeen, as also at Salford. Whereas most universities claimed high A level intake scores and heavy over-subscription for places a few laid claim to diversity of intake and still fewer wrote of value added.

Enterprise featured, usually with reference to an EHE programme. One institution (only) adopted the uncompromisingly managerial language more common in the PCFC sector, concentrating on managerial reshaping led by a 'Chief Executive'. It presented its objectives in terms of '(a) clients; (b) activities; (c) capture and use of financial resources', this last expression being twice repeated in the relevant sub-section, which also wrote of a management structure 'nimble enough' to exploit market opportunities, and of 'additional sophistication' in financial operations. Another university made a point of stating that its evolutionary managerial changes 'antedated Jarratt'.

As well as avoiding the term mission a few universities gave little sense of the kind of institution they wished to become – other than somewhat larger and more financially secure. Aberystwyth was not one of these:

> we have a clear vision of the kind of institution we aim to be. It will combine quality in teaching and research, a strong sense of community and a distinctive personality deriving from our size, our setting, the advantages accruing from neighbouring research institutions, and our admixture of cultures.

Aston was no less clear:

> Its superordinate objective is to be a leading technological university . . . . In its pursuit of excellence in the education that it offers, Aston places emphasis upon quality rather than quantity . . . . Aston is emerging as a quality-driven, demand-led institution, and is establishing for itself a distinctive place within the university sector.

Bradford, on the other hand, claimed strength

> in its openness to change and its ability to achieve it rapidly from a base of medium size, applied emphasis and relative youth. Bradford has a strong track record in the widening of access, continuing education, innovative teaching and the development of courses designed in particular to fit students for life and employment in the world outside.

Salford, to take one other new technological university,

> is a relatively small institution and consciously limits its areas of activity. The University's clearly defined purpose in teaching is to supply British industry and commerce with a body of educated, well-trained, and able graduates.

Salford first codified its aims and objectives in 1982. Its (annexed) revised version was headed 'The Responsive University'.

Kent did provide a mission statement:

in pursuing aims which it has in common with other universities – the maintenance of high-quality teaching and the promotion of research – the University intends making a significant contribution to the well-being and prosperity of society.... The University also plans to develop a high quality service of training, research and consultancy, in order to help meet local and regional needs, both by itself and in collaboration with other institutions.

The 'three legs' of teaching, research and community service, usually better balanced in North America than Britain, are evident here, and more clearly still in Exeter's 'three main Aims – Research and Scholarship, Teaching and Learning, and Service outside the University'. Other universities identified the three legs, if less clearly, Leeds for instance in adding 'meeting the needs of our students and of society' to undergraduate and postgraduate teaching and research.

Other universities also present this community service role as central, and not in conflict with academic excellence. Thus

The University's most distinctive feature is its ability to combine academic excellence over a very broad field ... and particularly in research, with a commitment to the community at regional, national and international levels, through continuing education, economic regeneration, the improvement of industrial competitiveness, and cultural development.... Our plans ... reflect our commitment to being a major research university which looks outwards to the wider community. (Warwick)

Manchester begins with its large size, breadth, popularity with applicants and employers, and research quality.

The University sees itself, however, less itself simply as an organisation with a leading national role in teaching, research and scholarship. It plays an important part in the life of Manchester and the North-West in many other ways.

For neighbouring Liverpool

the nature of its academic portfolio and a location at the heart of its city and region, have enabled the University over the last decade to play a significant role in the regeneration of Merseyside through the provision of short courses, consultancy services and technology transfer; active involvement in the development of Access courses to improve the very low age-participation rate [*sic*] in the region; and the availability of research and expertise through the expansion of its important activities in Urban and Regional Studies.

Similarly Southampton, while asserting its high research standing,

will continue to play a vital role in the continued cultural and economic prosperity of central Southern England. It has a long tradition of service to the local community through its programmes of liberal adult education and vocational continuing education, its involvement with professional and community agencies and its support for the arts.

In the north-east, Newcastle, one of the UK's largest academically broad universities,

> recognises its calling to further knowledge and understanding in the broadest sense and in a global context. More particularly and pressingly, however, the University of Newcastle is dedicated to serving a nation .... Any large British university might regard itself in this way. The University of Newcastle, however, also finds itself in a region of Britain that has pressing social and economic needs .... [In] our own work and in our active and intimate links with a concentric series of other institutions both public and private ... we are constantly concerned to maximise benefits for our own neighbourhood.

Community service, including continuing education, is not a monopoly of new or technological universities, or of civic universities in depressed industrial zones. Oxford's first long-term aim is 'to ensure that its standing as a world-class university is maintained and enhanced in both teaching and research', but two of its other six long-term aims are

> (5) to be more widely accessible, both by broadening recruitment to its degrees and by the expansion of high quality post-experience vocational and adult education courses....

> (7) to maintain close collaboration with industry and the professions in pursuing research and to ensure that the fruits of that research are made available to outside bodies both for commercial exploitation and for the benefit of society.

Oxford's rival and twin was more traditional in its five summary aims, though with mention of mature students and the needs of the community. Cambridge's nine pages on nature, aims and purposes do, however, include prominent and substantial sections on access, on continuing education and on links with industry and commerce. Later there are sections on its participation in other areas of society, its regional and local role, and collaboration with other areas of higher education. This is hardly the sketch of an archetypal ivory tower. But nor, like Oxford and for that matter Warwick or Southampton, is Cambridge a university that needs to scratch around for a plausible and distinctive identity.

Planning and managing change

Many of these institutional sketches are sharply at variance with what has come to be regarded as the traditional model: elite teaching and frontier research. Often continuing education is quite explicit. Others refer more loosely to local or community needs and service. However, one looks almost in vain for any *explicit* notion of lifelong learning, however convincingly it can be deduced from the statements. Leicester's preamble, exceptionally, states that

the University believes that the traditional university ideal of a liberal education and the contemporary emphasis on relevance in teaching and research are not incompatible and will continue to express this recognition through the range and quality of its work. The Government notion of 'education throughout life' is fully endorsed and finds expression in the University's proposals for expansion in the provision of continuing education.

The phrase 'education throughout life' is then taken up in the more detailed consideration of aims and strategies that follows.

Most universities, in addressing the task examined above, got down quickly to 'answering the question'. Sir Eric Ash, Rector of Imperial, allowed himself the indulgence of a brief foreword which reflected on the product and the process themselves:

A university plan must combine the individual aspirations of academic departments with the global purposes of the entire institution. Both aspects are exercises in foretelling the future – an activity which was recognised as less than totally reliable, even before the discovery of chaos. Whilst therefore we have produced a plan for four years, we regard planning as a continuous activity in which the differences between conjecture and the unfolding of reality can be rapidly identified and absorbed.

One can plan 'top-down' or 'bottom-up'. Our emphasis has put much of the emphasis on the latter.

It is in this spirit of reflective realism, rather than of cynicism on the one hand or naivete on the other, that we best read universities' Planning Statements. They tell us much about what universities wish in future to be, and how they hope to get there; but these are moving targets on a rolling screen. Will the correlation be high between the amount of 'bottom-up' planning and the closeness of aim to outcome? Yes, if universities remain largely collegial. No, perhaps, if managerial models win out.

We have seen how sensitive British universities have become to their national and local environments: to the needs of the regional economy and community as well as to the Aims of the UFC. The local environment is nowhere more sensitive and problematic than in Northern Ireland. This is how the Queen's University of Belfast began its Statement:

Universities play many parts. They advance knowledge, civilise societies, educate young school leavers and mature students, are a source of scientific, technical, professional and managerial skills needed for the betterment of mankind, provide a forum for debate, and enrich the lives of individuals by the nurturing of scholarship. They are, above all, centres of learning. For a century and a half the Queen's University of Belfast has been a civilising influence in a divided society. It has educated great numbers of men and women for the professions and at the same time has been part of an international community of learning. These roles will not change in the future. The University will continue to serve as a source of reconciliation and to maintain and enhance its contribution to the people, economy and society of Northern Ireland; at the same time it will extend its contributions to the world of scholarship by striving for excellence in teaching and research.

'These roles will not change in the future.' Is this then a conservative statement? Or do older purposes not often allow for, if not directly encompass, the different intentions contained in much of the 'new discourse' of Chapter 2? In Britain we are said to change things but to keep old names the same. Perhaps it is not the aims and purposes that need altering but the practical detail of how these are filled out?

Gradualism may be unacceptable to a Government impatient over access, relevance and economy; but universities have further time horizons than elected Governments. Gradualism may in fact pick out the route to a new identity and role for what in 1991 we call universities, in a greatly expanded HE system. On the other hand, listen to the calls for a new kind of partnership with industry (CIHE 1987); for significantly widened access (Ball 1990); for initial two-year degrees as one means to this, put forward by the Leverhulme seminars in 1983, echoed in a Leverhulme 'Reassessment' meeting at Birkbeck in 1990, and aired again subsequently in the *THES* (30 November 1990) and the *Guardian* of 9 April 1991. Even without making comparison with the more rapid expansion of the PCFC sector, or abroad with North American, Australian, French, Japanese or Scandinavian approaches, do these Planning Statements suggest optimal change or, rather, too conservative a preference for continuity?

4 | Out of the Box – Continuing Education University-wide

The elusiveness of university continuing education

> Universities in general have a weak hold on the need for more continuing education.

Richard Hoggart's observation, made when he demitted the post of Chairman of the Advisory Council for Adult and Continuing Education (ACACE) was cited by Johnson, Chairman of the UGC Continuing Education Working Party, in 1984 (UGC 1984b: ii). The generalization, directed essentially at the UK, had validity internationally. By then the concept of and discourse on lifelong learning and recurrent education were well over a decade old, but had taken little root in universities.

The search for a broader vision among the UK universities cannot be restricted to what they say to the UFC in seeking funds from the continuing education 'box'. We have to look beyond that administrative category for clues garnered elsewhere in universities' plans. Continuing education has for the moment come to have a particular administrative use which is narrower than its commonly held meaning. The narrow meaning has some utility, but it is too narrow a basis for asking about universities' development towards becoming lifelong learning centres.

The somewhat arbitrary and changing way in which increasingly large elements of the teaching effort of universities can be defined as CE or non-CE is at the heart of this chapter. There are developments which are not categorized for financial and administrative purposes as CE, but which demonstrate increasing flexibility and diversity. Taken together and projected forward a few years, perhaps to the end of the present planning period in 1995, they begin to suggest a more than token shift towards regional community service and recurrency of teaching provision.

It is the possible connectedness, or synergy, between different apparently piecemeal changes that may make them really significant: the whole may exceed the sum of the parts. In this chapter I turn first to modularization along with credit accumulation and transfer (CAT); then to mature age students and part-time degrees; and then to relationships between universities and other educational providers in their localities. Perhaps, with partnership a keyword, the road leads to lifelong learning *networks*, with universities as resource centres within these.

I leave for separate consideration in Chapter 6 the larger and more visible policy development under the name of Access. Before then I consider in Chapter 5 how compatible the old and new paradigms might be when it comes to combining traditional and non-traditional clienteles and their programmes. Part-time degrees come into the discussion as both a linked and a separate matter, and at graduate as well as undergraduate levels. Flexibility is the keyword here. Should we be referring not to full- and part-time degrees but, rather, to variable pacing?

There was little reference in universities' planning statements (Chapter 3) to lifelong learning, although other new concepts and terms have begun to invade the world of higher education (see Chapter 2). Britain is notoriously pragmatic and anti-philosophical, at least in OECD seminars on recurrent education and the like. Digging beneath the surface, however, can we discern real shifts in universities' visions, their concepts of themselves, which move away from the 'ivory tower', still used as a term of abuse?

An alternative 'community service station' model is implied by many of the planning statements to the UFC, although one might not be thanked for using such a term. It may carry unacceptable implications for the creation of a research agenda determined by the felt needs of 'the community' rather than by intellectual curiosity at the frontier of the discipline. Acknowledging a *de facto* shift from initial towards recurrent education may, however, by now come more easily.

In the education system at large, the *de facto* mainstreaming of adult education is an acknowledged fact:

> Educational provision for adults is no longer identifiable as separate from the mainstream work of further and higher education. Education for adults is changing as a result of the increased number of adults in further and higher education, the growing demand for retraining and updating, the emphasis on developing progression routes for those in adult education and structural changes among adult education providers themselves.
>
> HMI 1991: 18

It would be expedient for universities now to 'come out' and broadcast such a shift. A university pronouncement of this kind could be unacceptable to what are now the polytechnics and to the Open University. These naturally see themselves respectively as prime providers of regional community-oriented education, and as the specialist provider of university education for adults. From these institutional perspectives specialization of function – keeping the present universities relatively small as nationally recruiting elite providers for eighteen-year-olds and pure research students – may look like good market segmentation.

The gains from anything approaching rigid categorization and market segmentation are, however, outweighed, taking a broader view, by the damaging divisiveness which this is likely to continue inflicting upon society. Perched as they are at the top of the hierarchy of formal educational provision, the established universities have great power for good or ill. They can widen participation and a sense of opportunity and success throughout the education system; or accentuate the competitiveness and exclusiveness whereby the success of a high-achieving minority is fed by the failure and often the alienation of the majority, who do not collect a set of high-grade GCE A levels from the sixth form.

The scope of adult or continuing education

How has the term CE come to be circumscribed for some purposes, yet much expanded for others? We saw in Chapter 1 that *continuing* had by the later 1980s largely replaced *adult* as the broad general term. Before then several bodies sought to widen its scope, in the spirit of the Faure Report (Faure *et al.* 1972). Unesco adopted a Recommendation on the Development of Adult Education at its Nineteenth General Conference Session, using the following definition:

> the term 'adult education' denotes the entire body of organised educational processes, whatever the content, level and method, whether formal or otherwise, whether they prolong or replace initial education in schools, colleges and universities as well as in apprenticeship, whereby persons regarded as adult by the society to which they belong develop their abilities, enrich their knowledge, improve their technical or professional qualifications or turn them in a new direction and bring about changes in their attitudes or behaviour in the twofold perspective of full personal development and participation in balanced and independent social, economic and cultural development.
>
> Unesco 1976: 2

This definition is useful: not just for demonstrating what happens when an international committee creates a definition, but for what it says of the range and diversity of adult (now continuing) education, and indirectly about the values and connotations which underlie and inform it. The box, like the box built by OECD to contain adult education, is large enough to hold almost anything.

Nearer to home, definitions tend to be brief and simple, but not less broad. Sargant *et al.* (1990) begin by recalling the Report of the OU's Committee on Continuing Education in 1976, chaired by Sir Peter Venables. Continuing education was 'education for adults which is normally resumed after a break or interruption often involving a period in employment' (Sargant *et al.* 1990: 9). ACACE also cited Venables, and then a 1980 DES discussion paper on continuing education:

Initial education can be defined as the continuous preparatory period of formal study, to whatever level, completed before entering main employment. Continuing education covers anything which follows.

ACACE 1982: 1

The ACACE Report stressed its breadth of definition, encompassing education and training, vocational and general, and all systematic learning:

The existing distinctions, often developed for organisational or funding purposes, are not necessarily important to adult students.... We are particularly concerned about the continued dominance of initial education: both because it takes so much of the available resources, and because of the implication that a single lengthy period of education in the early years of life is expected to meet the changing needs of people throughout their lives.

ACACE 1982: 2

The influence of administration and funding are acknowledged – perhaps as a necessary evil. A decade later ACACE's concern about the resource hunger of initial *higher* education is echoed again. Now the demographic downturn which was expected to starve HE of young applicants and improve the chances of older, Access and part-time students is being cancelled by rising demand from the smaller eighteen plus age cohort, and as public resources to support students in HE continue to be concentrated on those studying in the full-time mode. (For the neglect of part-time student support, and the myopia which this betrays, see Tight 1991.)

Continuing education under the UGC and the UFC

The UGC (1984b), in the major report on continuing education and universities mentioned at the beginning of this chapter, also took a wide definition:

For the purpose of this study we adopted a wide definition of continuing education, describing it as 'any form of education, whether vocational or general, resumed after an interval following the end of continuous initial education'. This wide definition was generally welcomed. Our study was therefore concerned with the commitment of universities to:

(a) full-time mature students (those starting undergraduate courses at age 21 or over, and postgraduate courses at age 25 or over)
(b) part-time degree or diploma courses
(c) extra-mural courses
(d) post-experience vocational education courses (PEVE).

The report proceeded to address all four kinds of provision, employing the term 'short courses' to include both (c) and (d) above (UGC 1984b: 1) The joint NAB/UGC statement *Higher Education and the Needs of Society*, issued in the same year, added a fifth higher education objective to those set out by Robbins in the 1960s: 'the provision of continuing education in order to facilitate adjustment to technological, economic and social change and to meet individual needs for personal development' (NAB/UGC 1984: 2).

The UGC Working Party might have set the stage for a paradigm shift from 'front-end-loaded' to 'recurrent education', while avoiding any such grandiose Continental terminology. However, the somewhat studious avoidance of *education permanente*, lifelong education etc. carried a cost. The use of 'short courses' is confusing, since this is often equated with PEVE rather than extramural work. It also betrays an administrative, provider-driven, preoccupation, and a quest for convenience in aligning future vision with past practice. The report perpetuated the oft-disowned general–vocational dichotomy, and carried forward a split between CE funded under that label and CE which goes on within initial teaching. It thus inadvertently stunted universities' latent identity as centres for lifelong learning. In trying to avoid one set of boxes, university administration led by the UGC became boxed in again.

In 1989 the UFC replaced the UGC. Its Aims explicitly included extending continuing education. However, it inherited CE as a category, with sub-categories. These tended to diminish CE and to separate it from other widening of universities' roles, albeit to protect specific CE work. A letter from the DES to the Chairman of the UFC charged the new Council with taking on

> one additional responsibility, namely the funding of university extra-mural departments in England and Wales which have hitherto had Responsible Body status and received grant-in-aid direct from the Department and the Welsh Office.

The letter referred later to the rapid advances that the UGC Report had put in the short courses box:

> Universities have also made rapid advances in recent years in developing continuing education, including professional, industrial and commercial updating (PICKUP), increasingly on a self-financing basis. The changed needs of the economy require these developments to be consolidated and enhanced. The Government looks to the Council to establish mechanisms which ensure that continuing education is taken fully into account in planning at both national and institutional level.
>
> DES 1988: 2, 4

This double compartmentalization naturally re-appeared when the UFC came to act on these injunctions. Circular letter 15/89 announced the new system of funding CE, effective for the 1990–1 academic year, which would integrate three strands of funding:

  i   the FTE-based grants for the various types of CE paid as an indicated part of block grant;

  ii   PICKUP and INSET grants;

   iii funding for extra-mural departments recently transferred from the
      DES and Welsh Office. (UFC 1989b)

CE was for the purpose of this funding to be as defined in the Continuing
Education Record or CER, to which universities made their annual short
course returns. CE according to the CER is

   courses for less than 9 months in full-time length or the equivalent of
   part-time study, whether leading to certification or not, for which fees
   are payable (or sponsorship available) whether these courses are offered
   within university premises or elsewhere.

                                                            UFC 1989b

   The letter referred to the desirable integration of CE with other teaching
and research, and with planning for these. The longer letter later that year
dealing with all funding and planning for 1991–2 to 1994–5 set out the
Council's particular concern to increase undergraduate numbers and research output while protecting quality in both, and 'in respect of continuing
education – to promote its development as an integral part of university
activity, to encourage innovation and to rationalise funding' (UFC 1989c: 3).
   The categorization was more complicated still: the UFC sought to adopt
the different categories of LAE recommended by the Official Working Party
Report on The Funding of University Extra-mural Departments. This separated 'LAE' from credit-bearing courses on the CER, Access courses and
courses for disadvantaged groups requiring a high level of central support
(Summers 1988: 6). These became categorized in the bidding system as
LAE, credit-bearing courses, Access courses, disadvantaged student courses
and other high-cost courses. All these non-vocational courses were identified
separately from the vocational courses, with INSET a distinct category
therein. (Continuing medical education was completely excluded for other
reasons.)
   This detailed breakdown within the general education category left a
technical question to be resolved about monitoring and accountability, since
the CER did not provide such detailed information. More importantly,
although logically on financial and political grounds, this perpetuated a
separation from continuing vocational education. CE which has occupational
intent is expected to attract higher fees, although we know that motivations
and outcomes of and for students often do not match the 'liberal' or 'vocational' intentions of providers and funding bodies.

Containing CE, or fostering change

Most seriously from the perspective of this book, these arrangements perpetuated the separation of education for adults taking place within the
'mainstream', and also informal support for learning that occurs outside
registered classes and makes HEIs 'learning resources', from what could be

totted up as CE. They thus obscure any broader shift within regular university education in the direction of recurrence and lifelong learning.

They leave another technical problem. This has to do with where work belongs and is counted, as degree courses come to be broken down, built up and made available on a piece-by-piece or modular basis. My own university recently saw the migration of a substantial volume of 'short course' CER work into the mainstream USR teaching returns. This was for the Integrated Graduate Development Scheme (IGDS), which comprises series of short intensive residential teaching events and workplace-based project work. Another university, trying to protect its CE portfolio from hostile interpretation and consequently a low level of support from the UFC, referred to a number of factors fertile for misunderstanding. One of these had to do with such 'leakage', the loss of student numbers from the CER to the USR:

> Indeed, the current leakage of short-course CET volume as it is converted into long-term, award-bearing CET, with the consequential fall in reported CER volume will increase, especially in key growth areas such as software engineering, social work or pharmaceutical technology, where employers and professional bodies keenly promote this conversion.

The separate and temporarily partly protected status enjoyed by (narrower) CE under the new UFC regime does not necessarily cut it off from related and wider issues, such as access, CAT and modularization. This is a matter of organization and management for each university to decide. The specialized CE department may serve to champion a particular idea of the university, or be fuelled as an engine deliberately to pull in a certain direction. (Some PICKUP Regional Development Agents, whose remit is only to extend PICKUP, have expressed concern that bids for CE development funds are too preoccupied with the process of modularization.) How far each EMD or CE department is able, and enabled, to go beyond the narrower CE brief into matters of institutional mission and organization change will vary from university to university.

I now take three areas of innovation in the wider sense of CE and examine the universities' stance on each. They are

- modularization and CAT (credit accumulation and transfer)
- mature age students and part-time degrees
- relationships with other educational providers in the locality.

Modularization and CAT

Modularization and credit accumulation and transfer have made quite remarkable recent and accelerating progress up the policy agenda of HEIs, although neither is new. Alan Howarth, Parliamentary Under Secretary of State, DES, quoted Peter Toyne's 1979 explanation of credit transfer at a conference on

CAT in 1991. The idea that students can build up credit through units of study towards a qualification at their own pace and on their own basis of need and selection is well established, particularly in the United States. Study and credit may be accumulated within the one institution or more widely; universally in principle, so long as there is agreed comparability of value for study completed and assessed – that is to say, a common tariff.

CAT has been developed in the polytechnics for several years and some institutions have won a national reputation for modularization and CAT. CAT may be concentrated on internal choice: flexibility of course offerings and freedom for students to assemble within the institution the degree or diploma programme best suited to their needs. Even within a single institution arranging CAT can be a substantial task. Wider portability and student mobility can be cumbersome to negotiate for student and institution alike, until regional, national and increasingly international credit-rating and CAT are established. Even so, several years ago Middlesex Polytechnic had more students completing than beginning a number of its programmes. Its CAT procedures made it a net importer of students.

The very idea of CAT implies a paradigm shift in educational provision and curriculum design: from the institution to the individual student. Instead of 'the degree course', which the institution determines and which the student follows from the beginning of day one to the end of year three, there is the notion of a range of educational opportunity from which each student chooses. CAT is an export from the more individualistic and market-driven North American society. It challenges the British archetype of an institutionally planned three-year programme through which an annual cohort of students moves together. The traditional model is criticized as inflexible or 'lockstep'; the CAT approach is disparaged as a smörgåsbord, or pick-'n'-mix.

The salience of CAT was demonstrated by a heavily subscribed conference on the subject arranged in Oxford by the Kellogg Forum in March 1991 under the title 'Learning without Walls'. Its high profile, senior level participation and transbinary and wider membership symbolized the coming of age of CAT. In an opening address the Parliamentary Under Secretary of State praised its 'greater flexibility for future learning and full recognition for previous studies'.

> Progress in this area has perhaps been slower than the early enthusiasts might have liked or expected. That is not surprising, given the range of issues involved . . . . I welcome the present discussions about a National Framework for the Recognition of General Academic Credit. With so much activity and development in the field of credit transfer I am sure that it is timely to consider the need for a more consistent approach . . . . Institutions have always operated their own arrangements for the admission of applicants presenting a range of vocational and professional qualifications – or offering no formal qualifications. What we are witnessing now is an enormous expansion in this traditional flexibi-

lity.... CATS [CAT Scheme] will help to demolish the myth that higher education is something that you do when you leave school, or not at all.

Howarth 1991

Deliberations in the CNAA's CAT Committee suggest that, radical as the implications are, perturbations so far caused by CAT and modularization are but the first murmurings of an approaching storm. A dilemma for the CAT Committee is whether to credit-rate by conventional academic criteria, which means courses taught and assessed in established ways – the time-serving approach, in the jargon. Promotion of learning outcomes (UDACE 1991) and the accreditation of prior experiential learning (APEL), fuelled in part by the development of NVQs in vocational education and training, offer a much more fundamental challenge than do modularization and CAT to the assumptions and practices of HE, FHE and indeed the whole education enterprise. 'I recognise that the accreditation of prior learning raises particular difficulties: standards need to be maintained and there must be consistency of quality.' (Howarth 1991: 4) The learning outcomes, APEL and related movements gathering force this decade also, paradoxically perhaps, support ideas of lifelong learning and RE, for they stress continuing *learning* by diverse means, rather than the classroom teaching emphasis of more formal ('time-serving') *education* (compare Illich and Verne 1976).

Modularization is virtually a prerequisite for CAT, and this means that the curriculum is organized into discrete elements. Each can be studied and then assessed in a self-contained way, as well as compared and weighed in value for CAT purposes. The predominant CAT scheme in Britain, the CNAA's CATS, was launched in 1986. This encompasses both general and specific credit. It allocates credit points at the different recognized (undergraduate and graduate) levels. The numbers of credit points reflect size and scope of module. Credit specific to a particular area is often required at one level before a student can attempt a more advanced course in that particular area of the subject. Some criticize modularization and CAT as creating chaos for institution and student. The approach is parodied as allowing anyone to take anything in combination with anything else. In fact the rating system, and the abiding right and duty of HEIs to ensure both support for students and coherence of the programme, give the lie to this criticism.

More substantial is the question whether modularization, with assessment by or at the end of each module, represents a diminution of standards – a dilution of academic currency commonly referred to as threatening the gold standard. The evidence is unpersuasive. Oxford, like London, examines at the end of the undergraduate degree and the student stands or falls on this cathartic occasion. The Cambridge tripos is an old modular degree in all but name. Courses are examined each year, so that final honours examine only the work attempted in the third year of study. Cambridge degrees are not of notoriously lower status.

Student choice is usually a more-or-less matter, rather than either-or. Few programmes allow no measure of choice. None the less, the change implied by modularization (and then CAT) is significant and may be substantial. It fundamentally challenges the established, non-recurrent, idea of a university education: breaking up the cohort or year-group and in principle individualizing study programmes. On the other side it clears the way for flexible, through-life study opportunities.

This is where the connection to CE becomes relevant, and why some universities have sought CE Development funds from the UFC to accelerate modularization. Courses modularized into free-standing units are easier to 'package' and re-schedule. They can then be made available to different combinations of students, both individuals and groups, working perhaps towards different final qualifications. What may be a building block to one or more degrees or diplomas may also be attractive on its own to others with no interest in the associated credit towards a later qualification: to people in the community or workplace who have a particular learning need.

HEIs are being pressed towards greater economy in the name of efficiency. The economies of scale which can accompany such arrangements may thus become attractive. More attractively to the lecturer with a passion for a specialized area within the subject, such arrangements may spell the difference between the viability and non-viability of that course, especially where numbers are low at the honours and graduate levels of hard-to-recruit subjects. There is another implication, and a source of not always overt resistance. Teaching may need to be re-scheduled to evenings, early mornings, weekends, vacations, perhaps into a part-distance mode, when and where non-traditional students, or combinations of traditional and non-traditional students, can be reached.

'Mainstreaming', the integration or embedding of CE, is part of Government policy and has also been adopted by many universities. Modularization and CAT offer the flexibility needed if HEIs are to reach those for whom study must be fitted between the demands of other, prior, life roles to do with work, family or community life. As more HEIs modularize and join CAT schemes more freely and fully, it may prove impossible for all but the most powerful universities to stand apart from the development. What is the evidence about modularization in the universities in the 1990s?

Wider adoption of modularization

In the UFC/CE bidding round for 1990–1, modularization was a prominent area for development. The UFC invited bids for normal ongoing provision of LAE type courses, and for research into continuing education, along with two kinds of development funds, distinguished as Development and Innovation. In the event this distinction proved too fine to be helpful, and in the next round these were combined simply as Development (or pump-priming). For 1990–1, perhaps two-thirds of all universities bid for some CE development funds towards modularization of courses on the grounds that this would enhance opportunities for CE by making more of the university's expertise available on a short course basis. In addition some fifteen sought research or innovation funds for work to do with modularization. UCACE bid successfully for funds for a three-year development project on the introduction and impact of CAT throughout the system.

Planning statements to the UFC in 1990 provide startling evidence of how far, and by British standards how rapidly, modularization has caught on. The impression is confirmed by an enquiry conducted for the CVCP among its members by the Vice-Chancellor of Bradford the same year. Three members in the CVCP survey (Buckingham, Cranfield, the OU) do not receive funds from the UFC, so the set of universities is slightly different. Out of the fifty-eight universities seven did not reply. To a question 'are you moving towards modularization in undergraduate courses?', thirty-nine replied that they were, either (thirty) without qualification or with some qualifier such as 'partially' or 'being explored'. Of the eleven replying in the negative (one other checked 'don't know') three mentioned postgraduate modularization and half of them indicated some present practice of or plans for modularizing undergraduate work by one means or another. The seven universities not responding can be picked up from planning statements to the UFC: six said they were definitely modularizing and one referred to introducing instead a course unit system. With regard to timing, the earliest modularization dated from the foundation of the OU in 1969, some modularization was a decade old and plans varied from completion in 1990 to completion by 1995. In summary, there is a quite remarkable picture of commitment to explore seriously and in most cases to push through complete modularization by over fifty of the fifty-eight institutions.

Planning statements give an essentially similar picture apropos both modularization and CAT. Eleven civic and redbrick universities expressed commitment to modularization and all but two to CAT. For English technological universities the scores were five and six out of eight, with another making a minor commitment to both. The older English universities are least likely to move in these directions, although Cambridge recorded commitment to CAT, with cautious ideas for some modularization via its CE work. London is a special case complicated by both federalism and the specialized nature of some schools, but a majority expressed commitment to CAT and a larger majority to modularization. In the Welsh system there was much less commitment, one for CAT and two or three for modularization. Three specialized graduate schools had gone or were going modular, but our interest here is in the tougher undergraduate level. Both Irish and all eight Scottish universities (albeit one cautiously) committed themselves to CAT, with two and seven respectively for modularization. One of the seven commented that this was long-standing in some fields: the trend may be accelerated by the move to develop systems of credit transfer, although modularization is not seen by senate to be an essential prerequisite of such schemes. All the new universities expressed commitment to both developments.

This bald summary gives nothing of the flavour of the statements.

Discussion of both CAT and modularization appeared, broadly, in two contexts. One was to do with making the institution more accessible to non-traditional, older, students. The association might be with reaching non-traditional clienteles by means of access programmes. The other was to do with curriculum renewal and enhanced flexibility as part of the development and renewal of teaching programmes. Because these shade into each other, many universities wrote about CAT and modularization in both contexts, but for some the emphasis was more on one or the other. Modularization of postgraduate courses was also frequently mentioned, sometimes by universities among the minority not planning or exploring undergraduate modularization. They are not included in this sketch, since work at this level tends already to be much less bound by tradition, and more open to learners' diverse prior experience.

It was noted earlier that many universities sought CE development funds for modularization. When we observe how high a proportion of all universities made favourable reference to modularization somewhere in their planning statements (usually in the fourth section, on teaching and learning) the number seeking CE funds for such work appears modest. On the other hand the number making firm commitment to both CAT and some substantial measure of modularization is impressive.

A sample of twenty-four UCACE members who answered an inquiry at the beginning of 1991 into how they managed their CE provides one more piece of evidence about the shift in these areas, and the connection with what each university recognizes as CE. Twelve of these universities recorded including CAT activity directly in their CE work, and fifteen answered similarly in respect of modularization. When the same question was asked about the university's broader idea of CE (rather than what the specialized department does) the numbers rose to twenty and eighteen. This corroborates the view: (a) that CAT and modularization are fast taking hold in the university sector and (b) that they are generally seen as intimately linked with CE, though not necessarily part of the responsibility of a specialized CE department.

Mature age students and part-time degrees

The UFC asked about the balance of full-time and part-time study and about increasing student access. Its Aims specify both full-time and part-time students and young and mature students. I return to the balance or mix between young and older students in the next chapter. It is convenient to separate this from modularization and CAT for purposes of analysis. In practice these are all part of a naturally related cluster of changes to do with flexibility and access, and all linked with CE.

Another distinction is necessary, but can also mislead. Scepticism about HEI self-interest can be set in opposition to values associated with access and flexibility – having a second chance, equality of opportunity. The values often travel these days, for convenience and security, in company with purposes about the economy, or about human resource development. Sound institutional self-interest tends to align with society's needs of its HEIs. However, it must also take account of government policy, which in principle represents the needs of society. On universities' longer time scales the dichotomy between institutional self-interest and society's needs largely dissolves.

Malcolm Tight's 1991 study of part-time degrees shows how ahistorical we can be about the idea of a university or of higher education; and how we can overlook what is happening even today – in this case the volume of part-time higher education – if it does not fit the prevailing paradigm. Government, like many of the other influences pressing upon higher education which characterize a mature, complex and plural society, demands more mature age access to degree courses and more part-time provision. Yet, trapped in an old paradigm, it fails to re-balance scales that are heavily weighted in favour of full-time residential undergraduates.

Universities sometimes share this blindness to what does not fit. Two examples are particularly revealing. One is the common blindness to precedents for part-time and mature age study, and to special entry at graduate levels – a *de facto*, half-acknowledged acceptance of life experience not hitherto often described as APEL. Gatekeepers and bouncers (the admissions tutors) are busy at the undergraduate front door; the back may be unguarded and half open. Secondly, there is ambivalence, again revealingly little noticed, about students in the region who can live at home and study locally – so powerful are the discourse, currency and performance indicator of A level scores, which imply competing nationwide for the best students. The common Scottish practice of going to your local university, also the norm for many in Australia, much of Continental Europe and North America, comes less readily to mind south of the Scottish border.

Do planning statements suggest any movement here? Or does the older non-recurrent, finishing school norm still absolutely prevail, in a country whose leaders still tend to go away, not just to university (rather than polytechnic) but before that to a private boarding school? Can students work their way through a degree programme at the local HEI at their own pace, permitting part-time employment and other activities? Or is this only for the second rate and the second class?

A few examples give a flavour of plans for mature age and part-time students. Among the civic and redbrick universities all but one of the fourteen make specific and unequivocal commitment to building up part-time undergraduate programmes and numbers. The one remaining case refers to a range of piecemeal access-type provision to assist non-traditional students into and through the first year, although apparently only on a full-time basis. It is not always clear whether percentage increases refer to aggregated undergraduate and postgraduate part-time numbers. Often references to part-time expansion are linked with statements about non-standard entry generally (that is, for full- *and* part-time students) or with observations about modularization and CAT.

One university includes among its objectives increasing its part-time student numbers from 530 to around 900 full-time equivalents (FTEs), doubling mature and non-standard entry numbers, and widening access and part-time provision through various access partnerships, modularization and CAT developments. Another, least sure about moving in these directions among this group, prefers 'degrees by extended study' to 'part-time' degrees. Manchester's 'degrees by degrees' programme had taken part-time students to 4 per cent of undergraduate FTEs and the number was set to rise faster than full-time numbers. There was strong emphasis on equal opportunity here – widening rather than merely extending access. Sheffield also stressed equal opportunity as well as rising non-standard entry, further part-time degree development, outreach work and the Mundella Programme involving partnership and CAT with FE. Another university had reviewed its admissions processes from an APEL perspective, introduced an incentive scheme to departments to teach part-time students in the evening and adapted other facilities to meet mature student needs.

One university committed itself to increasing its mature numbers from 9 to 14 per cent of intake; another already takes 17.5 per cent mature students and has quotas in many subjects. Elsewhere mature and non A level students are analysed by subject area (ranging from 10.8 to 27.5 per cent): 'the success rate of such students is high and we intend to increase recruitment from these categories'. It was also said that 'modularization will permit many more undergraduate courses to be taken by part-time study'. Elsewhere again

> a number of the University's module-based first degree programmes are taken on a part-time basis with assessment geared to a credit accumulation system. At present only a small proportion of undergraduates are registered for part-time study.... The University expects to see an increase in the number of part-time students by 1995 and will take this into account in the revision of course structures, with particular reference to the development of access courses linked to conventional degree programmes.

At another civic university there were already 989 mature undergraduate students (FTE). Plans were well advanced for part-time general degree programmes which would give eligibility to Honours after three years' equivalent full-time study, with intermediate qualifications after one and two years. Target numbers were also given. Elsewhere part-time degrees started in 1988; the policy is to expand such schemes, some in association with other HEIs in the region. Finally, a redbrick university

> is rapidly expanding its part-time course provision at both undergraduate and postgraduate levels in response ... to growing mature student demand .... The University intends to explore the potential for expanding part-time/evening degree course provision and hopes, in particular, to develop courses which will meet the needs of the large Asian community.

This is just one of a number of (especially) city universities which specify minority ethnic and other groups identified according to equal opportunity criteria, for whom access to degrees will, it is hoped, be widened.

These illustrations are taken from one subset of UK universities, the civics and redbricks, partly because of their geographical location, partly because they are seen as the 'heartland' of the British system. They slightly exaggerate the general level of aspiration towards diversified provision to reach local adults, but the overall picture is not markedly different. Not all the ex-colleges of advanced technology are moving into part-time undergraduate work: for them the strong sandwich tradition represents a different form of 'non-traditional' study. Five out of seven English plateglass institutions are doing so, with a sixth considering it. All but one technological university and all the new universities express commitment to widening access to non-traditional mature students. The London system includes a number of commitments to both part-time and expanded mature undergraduate students, but the old collegiate universities are, unsurprisingly, not committed to undergraduate part-time work, apart from Oxford via its continuing education operations at first-year level. Oxbridge and Durham do write about some extension of mature entry, however. Outside England, five Welsh colleges make commitments to expand mature entry as do the two Northern Ireland institutions and all eight Scottish universities. On part-time degrees the respective numbers are four, two and six.

We have, then, a picture of almost universal commitment to the principle of widening access to mature full-time students. Often there is also explicit commitment to attracting lower socio-economic and minority ethnic groups, and to attracting women into science and technology. Around three-quarters of all universities make some commitment to starting or expanding part-time undergraduate courses and numbers.

Relationships with other providers

Another aspect of becoming centres for lifelong learning (outside CE in the administrative sense) concerns universities' local external relations. Partnership with industry, for example as promoted by CIHE (see Chapter 3), heralds a radical shift towards a learning society in which education is acknowledged to be lifewide as well as lifelong. What about partnership with other educational institutions? The UFC's Aims call for 'increasing collaboration between universities and other institutions of higher and further education'. Detailed notes to Circular letter 39/89 ask that planning statements have in mind 'relations with schools and the further education sector' and 'collaboration with other higher education institutions'. I leave aside relations with schools, principally open days, visiting and other recruitment efforts to win a share of sixth-formers. What have the statements to say about a set of formal relationships with other HEIs and especially with FE colleges, which may facilitate entry, transfer and general mobility within the FHE system?

The words to look for are affiliation, consortia, including the Authorised Validating Agencies (AVAs) for Access courses, and, especially, franchising and validation. One form of relationship that goes beyond franchising is known as 'two plus two': an arrangement whereby FE and HE jointly plan and offer open entry programmes leading to an honours degree in four years, two in each kind of institution. Taken together with modularization, CAT and clearer recognition of one's locality again, as a primary source of students, these networking arrangements could transform HEIs into centres within regional learning consortia which move educational provision nearer to supporting a 'learning society'.

Arithmetical analysis is probably unhelpful, and space precludes a full account of the different arrangements described and foreshadowed in the statements. The large picture is one of very considerable association of various kinds. Involvement in access consortia, usually by 1991 via AVAs, is widespread. In Scotland there is the Scottish Wider Access Programme (SWAP). A number of universities have validation arrangements with institutions that are in some kind of formal or informal affiliation or association. These enable students to gain university qualifications through other colleges – and so provide another form of enhancing access to the course awards of universities. Validation seems to be spreading rapidly. The drive behind it may well be partly territorial imperialism in the sense of creating special relationships and magnetism for students, particularly in the local region, but the result can be to create a regional lattice-type access system into which the validating HEI is woven. The impact of the 1991 Further and Higher Education White Papers (DES 1991; Clarke *et al.* 1991) is likely to be an accentuation of this trend.

A small number of universities set out more ambitious and specific partnership arrangements and plans, some on 'two plus two' lines. Outside this are the several universities that franchise their access or foundation courses to FE colleges (as distinct from validating colleges' courses). A redbrick university claims major success for a two plus two scheme that 'permits the entry of students with industrial or similar experience to a two-year ITT [initial teacher training] course'. Another university has initiated (as an industrial, not an FE, partnership) an intensive one-year course for employees without experience of HE which can 'provide a fast route to a standard normally reached at the end of six terms'. This can result in a completed degree in one more year full-time, or longer part-time. Its scope is to be widened, it is hoped, to other industrial partners. A Scottish university has links with institutions offering HNC and HND (higher national certificate and diploma) qualifications, and a scheme for exemption for up to two years of a four-year honours degree. In the other direction, an English civic writes of sub-contracting first-year courses to local FE colleges.

Lancaster's heavy involvement in its region, especially through the Open College of the North-West, is well known, and it refers to identifying with FE colleges areas of demand for particular part-time programmes to extend its partnership and credit-transfer arrangements (which include the OU).

Another new university, Warwick, is developing a two plus two scheme with local FE colleges, with target numbers for different subject areas. Salford's established two plus two scheme is set out to the UFC in some detail. When the statement was drawn up the university had 300 students on eight courses involving four colleges. A variation was a one plus two IT degree, and eight colleges were affiliated to a scheme due to get fully under way in 1990. Finally, two Welsh university colleges mention two plus two. One plans to move to an HND-based scheme 'in association with the local tertiary sector'. The other has planned two plus two links with an Institute of Higher Education.

How significant will these local FHE relationships become? Will they be left mainly to the ex-polytechnic universities rather than the older universities, as an article in the *THES* (28 June 1991) seemed to imply? Partnership is a delicate business: paternalism and imperialism can be felt when they are not intended. Will institutional competition enhance separatism, or will the gains from collaboration, joint planning and marketing, and linked provision, be seen to outweigh it? The Editor of the *THES* proposed such regional collaboration – blurring rather than sharpening the line between FE and HE – at a seminar in Oxford in 1990, and in a subsequent *THES* leader. The theme has been amplified by the Vice-Chancellor of Warwick, Clark Brundin, drawing on Californian experience.

Does what universities say they are planning suggest a paradigm shift? Maybe. Look, however, at what the CIHE says about partnership; at what the RSA says about more meaning different; at the UDACE work on learning outcomes; at the Leverhulme case for two-year degrees; at the NCVQ's competency approach to vocational education; and at the idea of shifting from elite to mass higher education. We may still then say, with universities' sterner critics, 'this is too little and too late'. Let us now probe further whether the traditional idea of a university education can coexist with this emergent paradigm.

5 | Finishing School or Service Station – What Mix?

The residential norm

The young full-time residential undergraduate is assumed to be the normal university student. Yet there are older full- and part-time students, and most HEIs have larger numbers of students on non-award-bearing CE courses than are enrolled for degrees. What mixes, especially of undergraduate students, may be comfortable, tolerable and also desirable for universities? Can the 'traditional' idea of a university education coexist with an emergent paradigm of HEIs as centres for lifelong learning? Or can non-traditional students be tolerated only as long as they are too small a minority to risk altering campus culture?

Remember that 'traditional' applies to contemporary British *notions* of a 'normal university education', not necessarily to past or present practice in Britain or abroad. In the next chapter I examine a related aspect: not the stress that heterogeneity may cause for HEIs, but the notions and measures of quality and success that may attach to students and teaching within the new access paradigm.

Over fifteen years ago part-time adults became the majority of Canadian university students (Campbell 1984: 14). Including adults studying full-time, those who in Britain are normally called mature age students, would have shifted the pre- to post-experience (or youth to adult) balance still further in favour of the latter. In Australia no distinction is made among students in the class. They may be young full-time students straight from school; people returning to study after a year or two out, before or within their degree course; much older students whose children sit as students alongside them and with whom they will later graduate; or young or older people working their way through a degree by taking one or two courses a year and earning at the same time. To a North American or Australian academic all are normal university students.

In British universities, and still perhaps in some polytechnics and colleges of higher education, this is not the case. A university is the place through which passes what Sir Eric Ashby once called the 'thin clear stream of excellence': the highest achieving eighteen-year-olds who study one of the disciplines owned and enhanced by an academic department of that name. A degree then represents a high level of intellectual attainment in that subject or preferably discipline, measured by class of honours attained over three years of full-time study.

Study is certainly 'residential' in the sense of being undertaken away from home, although not every such student can be found a place in a college or hall of residence. Making a virtue of necessity, the challenge of living away from home and learning to cope becomes part of the young person's *rite de passage*. However, university planning statements for the 1990s spell out aspirations to build more undergraduate residential accommodation on one financial basis or another. Some also attempt a principled shift or a pragmatic slide into the new access paradigm: plans to expand numbers of part-time and other home-based students will lead to better use of existing capital plant, reducing the pressure to build more residential accommodation.

In displaying this ambivalence universities reflect an ambiguity located deeper in society and its education system. GCE A level examinations are commonly criticized as being too narrow, too specialized, and too powerful and negative an influence over aspiration to proceed to higher education. They are staunchly defended by successive Secretaries of State for Education. The same term, the 'gold standard', is used as is used about the British honours degree system. As we will see in the next chapter, universities make play of their competitive exclusiveness, measured by the number of qualified A level holders they turn away. To win in the 'aggregate A level points' stakes HEIs must attract students nationwide, i.e. into a residential, or at least a living-away-from-home, mode.

The success of polytechnics in this annual contest is measured less perhaps in A level scores, since the polytechnics labour under a considerable disadvantage of status, and more through stories of the triumph of ingenuity over adversity and deprivation. Seaside holiday camps are requisitioned along with camp beds in church halls and gymnasia to sleep the overspill of young people living away from home with no Oxbridge college bed and bedder to give them comfort. The combination of residentiality and competitive entry is nowhere more clearly and ironically marked. It is not surprising that these other HEIs, aspiring to university status and conditions, want to play by common rules. So a 'real university' and a 'real degree' in the full-time residential paradigm retain their hold even in HEIs that are more confidently anchored in the newer access world.

Programme and student diversity

It is similar for the course of study. One generation of British universities, the ex-colleges of advanced technology, make virtue of their sandwich provision, involving industrial placement, often for a full year within a four-year degree. The links with industry which this gives are naturally claimed to enhance the 'relevance' of study and subsequent employability. Another subset, the new universities of the 1960s, tend to make more of their flexibility and interdisciplinarity than do the older foundations, although these two terms have wide currency through most of the planning statements for 1991–2 to 1994–5. Yet the template from which variations are developed remains the single or perhaps the joint honours degree, with combined studies and other variations still finding little more than a toe-hold in universities' new teaching–learning aspirations.

In other words a new paradigm manifests itself in the planning and language of access, continuing education, flexibility and partnership; yet the three-year residential honours degree, instinctually and scarcely acknowledged, owned by and based in a disciplinary department, retains its stranglehold. This hold is the more powerful: (a) for being unacknowledged, taken for granted rather than explicitly stated; (b) because it aligns with deep-seated elitism in a society which values competitiveness and exclusiveness. It is reinforced by government policies and pronouncements affecting all parts of the education system. The tension between elitism and wider human resource development in national policy-making naturally finds echo in the universities, and in what they say in trying to win resources from government for their work. In a few cases institutions seek to square the circle completely. They claim for the collegiate model of education special virtue and success in terms of the new terminology of competences and personal transferable skills described in Chapter 2.

Universities are pluralistic 'non-organisations'. How much diversity of values, purposes and activities can they tolerate? Can the old and new paradigms – the thin clear stream of excellence and the broad flood of access – run together through the same campuses and faculty boardrooms? Aston University, like Salford in its different way, sustains a clear and distinctive profile or mission, which was made public and well known during the 1980s. Many of the planning statements, however, to put it one way, hedge their bets. Two sets of values and kinds of discourse sit together within the one set of covers. There is not always much reconciliation. The magnetism of a gentle cathedral city setting measured by heavy UCCA overbidding among school sixth-formers, and the high A level scores of those admitted, is set beside a commitment to attract more mature age students, to begin or extend part-time degrees, to widen the institution's social, gender or ethnic intake.

A few universities are explicit about managing such diversity. Warwick asserts in opening its planning statement that

> the University's most distinctive feature is its ability to combine academic excellence over a very broad field . . . with a commitment to the community . . . . Our plans for the period up to 1994 reflect our commitment to being a major research university which looks outwards to the wider community.

Many of the statements, though less explicit than this, do suggest that they will remain, or become more, eminent in research terms while heeding UFC aspirations for a larger and more open university system. On the other hand there is much discussion, not only in continuing education departments, about the competition for precious academic staff time: between research, different forms of teaching, and community service.

The argument about the binary divide has been partly a debate about *system* diversity: can the HE system be unified and yet more variegated within it? 'Ironically, unitary systems can sometimes have steeper institutional hierarchies than binary ones' (CNAA 1991 : 1). Conversely, the university system, which is 'unitary plus the Open University', looked likely to be pushed into a tripartite division of status and funding in the late 1980s. There would then have been three categories of universities, R, T and X (research, teaching only and mixed status). This league table of universities was not then created, and access to research funds remains problematic as some funds are moved from the UFC to the research councils. Differentiating out research-only universities is suggested from time to time (see the *THES* main leader of 29 March 1991).

Not all institutions are explicit in claiming to combine academic excellence and community service. They do all indicate some contribution to newer as well as traditional forms of teaching. Some statements identify a natural link between research and continuing education, enabling state-of-the-art research to be rapidly disseminated and applied where relevant. The rationale for adding non-traditional students to universities' spectrum of aims and activities is not expressed in this way, but rather in terms of national and UFC policies and aims, which are echoed in the statements. A few explain technical arrangements for widening access: a kind of bounty payment to encourage departments to recruit part-time students; evening teaching to increase the use of capital investment.

Any relationship between non-traditional (older or part-time) and traditional teaching of young students with conventional A levels appears not to be addressed. Perhaps it is not seen as an issue. If so the concerns and criticisms of the 'access movement', for instance the Forum for Access Studies (FAST) and the Open College Networks (OCNs), look to be well founded: that HEIs expect new kinds of students to fit themselves into existing arrangements, rather than seriously to adapt their teaching and student support services to new kinds of needs.

Integrated and separate provision

To whom do students 'belong'? Sweatshirts and degrees bear the name of the university. For the student, as for the lecturer, primary loyalty is often to department and subject; and in some universities, ancient and modern, also to the hall or college. Barnett goes so far as to ask whether students taking different courses are 'in effect in separate institutions of higher education, closed off from each other' (Barnett 1991; see also Barnett 1990). Part of the resistance to modularizing academic programmes stems from a fear that students will become academically lost: disoriented impulse buyers of ill-matched baskets of goodies from the supermarket shelves. Resistance to accelerating wider access comes from some admissions tutors struggling to select, often from massive over-supply, a quota of high-fliers to fit the culture, aspirations and expectations of their departments.

Contrast the 'negotiated curriculum' with the 'class of '79'. In the former, each student enters into a 'learning contract' with the institution, agreeing a curriculum to meet individual needs and interests. In practice it will not be an open choice but a possibly modest measure of pick-'n'-mix within the framework set by the institution. CAT within the institution using a common 'tariff' makes it easier for students to range beyond one departmental home. The contract is with the HEI rather than, effectively, with one department. The class of '79 who enter, live and learn together then looks more like the traditional primary school class than its more adventurous successor.

A modular curriculum and CAT quickly affect the teaching timetable. They may force the institution into more flexible, varied, including self-directed, forms of learning and teaching, as students move around to find the resources for their needs in different ways, rather then travelling as one intake. Again the more tidy, familiar world of the subject teacher and disciplinary scholar in the department crumples.

It is unclear how far these consequences have been recognized. The impression is that they have not; and that implementing plans in the next several years will cause strains and set up dissonances of the kinds suggested above. As these strains are felt, there will be efforts to revert to the familiar norm of homogeneous, department-managed 'cohort teaching'. This is evident already in some universities, and reportedly too in the polytechnic sector. It is fed by each announcement that the 'demographic timebomb' of falling birth cohorts failed to explode and depress demand for HE (Smithers and Robinson 1989). The 'battle of the modules' may soon be engaged in earnest. It will be especially interesting to see how the (attractive but labour-intensive) individualized tutorial system, which several collegiate institutions emphasize in their statements, fares in this environment. The costly Oxbridge system is at the heart of the British university ideal – the golden core of the gold standard. Unimaginatively handled, the tutorial system will be squeezed to death as 'productivity' is pushed up and staff–student ratios deteriorate in this most labour-intensive of industries.

Tackled with imagination and courage, it could, as some statements do suggest, allow an institution (or its colleges) to provide individualized learning support to new kinds of (alias non-traditional) students on more self-directed study programmes built up out of the newly modularized curriculum, with more overt attention paid to the transferable skills and competences of the 'new discourse'. The Training Agency's Enterprise in Higher Education (EHE) initiative to which many planning statements refer requires the attitudes and skills of 'enterprise' to be integrated into the curriculum of all students, not just a non-traditional minority. This implies a *synthesis* of old and new, not some juxtaposition of essentially different, merely coexisting, species.

A case can be made for teaching young and older students separately. The pragmatic short-term argument is, however, outweighed by longer-term considerations. The case is that adult students' learning needs, and perhaps too the needs of different disadvantaged minorities, are so different that they are better catered for quite separately; and that HEIs are too inflexible to change sufficiently to accommodate new kinds of learners' needs. Some countries sustain institutes of adult education for the separate education of adults. Further education colleges may provide their Access courses for adult returners in a special annex where these older students can feel more at ease – or are they, rather, ghettoized second class students? Herein lies the tension. Some special needs may demand separate special provision. Yet putting adults permanently into separate arrangements may, like putting handicapped children into special schools, stigmatize them, labelling them different and inferior. It is difficult to be separate and different, but equal.

The dilemma is manifested by the seven long-term residential colleges, from Ruskin to the most recently founded, Northern. They have come to be seen as part of the higher education system specializing in effect in access courses for the educationally disadvantaged and commonly feeding people into regular degree programmes, rather than as a separate form of provision, complete and valid in itself. The case for separate, specialized and highly professional adult education would be defended against the view that regular HEIs should make this provision in the normal way. The benefits of immersion in learning via residential education away from family and community pressures are also pointed out, compared with day-time Access courses offered by local FE colleges. Scotland's only long-term residential college, Newbattle Abbey, has been closed on the ground of extravagance. In a poignant seminar exchange at Oxford, Ruskin's residential provision was criticized by the former head of an Oxford college as being indefensibly costly. The irony was not lost on Ruskin's Principal, Stephen Yeo. He pointed out how seldom the same criticism was made of the costly education of the Oxford colleges themselves, provided for those who, in terms of advantage, often least need it!

What is the most efficient and economical balance between integrating wider access students into 'mainstream' provision, and making separate provision? For how long and at what cost should there be separate provision? What are the educational as distinct from administrative objections to rethinking the curriculum and pedagogy of the university from the perspective of the non-traditional student – as EHE requires its beneficiary institutions to do from another perspective?

The separation of andragogy from pedagogy as a distinct professional discipline has exaggerated the differences between teaching younger and older people. It draws an artificially sharp line between the learning of young adults at eighteen and that of those over twenty-one, called mature students. Without this separateness, and the historic marginalization of adult from pre-experience education, the question of a tension or balance between (traditional) young and (non-traditional) older students might never have arisen.

In practice it must be admitted that the old paradigm governs most British universities old and new. The normal, real, university undergraduate is the eighteen-year-old finishing his or her education, whether from a private boarding school or from the newer meritocracy of a state grammar or comprehensive school. A partial exception is the technological universities with their strong tradition of sandwich education. No wonder the access movement stresses widening (and not merely increasing) access.

Britain decided in the late 1960s to provide part-time adult university degree-giving education through a separate TV University or University of the Air, eventually called the Open University. This was resented by some university extramural departments as taking bread out of their mouths – not that they gave their students access to a degree or even at that time to the first rungs on a degree ladder. On the other hand it *was* separate, and it was certainly seen, well into the eighties and not just when it was founded at the end of the sixties, as letting regular universities off the hook: part-time provision and mature age entry were 'not our job', being the business of the OU. By contrast, when Australia appointed a committee to look into creating an open university in the 1970s it was decided to foster openness throughout the system and not set up a separate institution.

Three distinct issues here intertwine. One is the *status* of separate educational institutions, and of the degrees which they award. Are non-traditional students better off in the mainstream of university provision, even though it is badly designed or adapted to meet their circumstances and needs? Another is atmosphere: the style or *culture* of the undergraduate experience. How far can it accommodate diversity of age, educational and social background, ethnicity and even gender? What benefits and possible losses are associated with greater heterogeneity? The third is the matter of *resources* and logistics. What is the impact, on budgets and administrations as well as departments and lecturers, of diversifying the student intake, mixing a service station role with that of the finishing school? I will address each of these issues in turn, then conclude this chapter by looking at what universities' planning statements may imply about them.

Status

Special purpose adult education institutions have been distinguished, and partly driven, by their values, which are social democratic and egalitarian as well as liberal. This is true for the Workers' Educational Association (WEA), the long-term residential colleges, and extramural departments within the universities. The WEA traditionally set its face against certificating study, the learning and the empowerment flowing from it being its own end. The colleges certificated their long courses. Although the value system was not dissimilar, they have always provided a route for some students into regular academic education, and so a form of access long before Access courses were invented. Access provided locally in FE is now used as one ground to question their continuing viability. The extramural departments have long awarded extension certificates and diplomas, although their validity and the legitimacy of the arrangement have been called into question (Duke and Marriott 1973).

Much has changed of late in the standing and certification of higher adult education. This is not the place to tell the story of extramural modernization, but one important trend has been to draw non-degree higher adult education into the common frame and currency, so that it gives access and increasingly shares status with the dominant, degree-giving HE system. Extramural certificates connect more with undergraduate degrees as an alternative form of matriculation, increasingly with 'advanced standing' or exemption from part of the undergraduate degree. Free-standing extramural certificates have little or no value for the individual. Being part of a social movement does not bring in the bacon; having a degree just might.

The status, or lack of status, of separate provision is clearly important. The OU provides an example, its status secured in various ways. The 'public sector' of polytechnics and colleges jostles for status with the older and more prestigious university sector. Within each sector there is jockeying for place on informal league tables of standing, and juggling to create new tables in which one's institution ranks high. The quality assurance mechanisms of newer institutions include external examiners from more prestigious places. New institutions are staffed from longer established places. They may emulate and often deliberately exceed the requirements laid upon students by higher status HEIs. CAT should reinforce the 'common currency' of all HE effort, insofar as polytechnic, OU, 'extramural' and even industry-based credit points can count towards a prestigious university degree.

A pecking order will persist. Scarcity has its value. Oxford and Cambridge will not greatly expand. Their degrees will not be confused with those of later twentieth-century foundations, least of all by employers who exercise a responsibility, via the PI of employability, as arbiters for a surrogate of quality. We can now locate the question of diluting or transforming the 'finishing school' in a wider context. If wider access is to have full and equitable meaning, trends towards integrated rather than separate provision must persist. There will in future be greater differentiation within the British degree system – departure from the gold standard perhaps. Such differentiation should be on the lines of need for different kinds of graduates and so output-related, not based on different kinds of recruits into higher education and so input-related. The 'society open to the talents' sought by free market economists no less than latter-day Tawneyite radicals cannot start by pre-determining which men (and nowadays also women) are of gold and which of baser metal.

There is, then, an *a priori* reason for resisting status differences within HE between traditional and non-traditional students. Differentiation should ideally relate only to *function*. It is socially undesirable because artificially divisive, and inefficient in human resource terms, if the lower status public sector has a virtual monopoly of non-traditional students and social groups, and if this sector, in adopting university status, yet remains a caste apart. This is the long-term significance for society of genuinely wider access in the universities.

Culture

One may argue *a priori* that service station and finishing school should combine, even in the most prestigious collegiate institutions. What does this actually mean for the culture of the classroom? Is it all gain, or are there serious stresses?

Three categories of people are affected: young undergraduates whose expectations and territory are partly invaded; non-traditional students who are initially an alien and insecure minority; and university staff, both the teaching staff and those in support roles from secretaries and porters to counsellors and careers advisers, who are also affected by change of intake.

The territory of the young is only partly invaded. Residential quarters – halls, colleges, digs – and even the student union facilities tend to be off bounds to older non-residential students, full- and part-time alike, unless by personal friendship and invitation. For those at finishing school the student role is commonly an all-encompassing one. Subsidiary roles, formal (union, sporting) and informal (daring, dating), often overshadow that of student-scholar. For all that a one-week OU summer school can be a socially as well as intellectually demanding and exciting experience, the more extreme manifestations of studenthood, such as the American hazing and fraternity rituals, sit furthest from the mature student.

For older students the student-scholar role has to be juggled into space cleared between other, imperative, roles, especially family supporter in economic and social senses. The common space shared by different kinds of students even on a traditional degree course may be quite small. Codes of conduct for coexistence in these few hours each week can be negotiated. The more the curriculum becomes modular, the less significant non-traditional students may be. Each class and course may be a new social and learning event in which each member starts as a temporary stranger on the same basis. In practice, existing university teaching situations spread along a broad spectrum between the class of '79 and a modular mix of strangers. The impact of student diversity also varies along it.

As far as I am aware little scholarly attention has been paid to this aspect of changing university life. Some small studies explore how young and older students mix and relate to one another (Field 1988, 1989; Gardner and Pickering 1991). Folk wisdom has it that the best advocacy of wider access comes from mature students in the system. They prove rewarding to teach and stimulating to younger colleagues who are often more intimidated by tutors and less clear and motivated in the student role. Youngsters may be inhibited by a student culture – an affectation of indifference, of being laid back. I have certainly found experience with older students the most persuasive argument within the university, in terms of job satisfaction in the classroom. Direct experience is usefully buttressed by research evidence of the performance of NSEs – non-standard entry students who have not come by the normal school route and matriculated with GCE A levels. The work of Bourner and others (see Bourner and Hamed 1987a, b) proves useful in support of advocacy; but the heart is won through experience, buttressed by evidence to satisfy the head.

Classroom culture is more complex than this implies. Departments familiar with mature age students, like applied social studies and more broadly the social sciences and humanities, need no persuading. They may have long enrolled a mature age majority of undergraduates year by year, as well as experienced professionals at graduate levels. There are, however, legitimate concerns about the desirable mix of young and older students; about the inhibiting as well as enabling effect that older students can have on shy nineteen-year-olds. Access proponents concerned for shy disadvantaged older people would be wise not to ignore this. I have colleagues who are pleased to take a large minority of mature age students into their courses, but resist the proportion reaching 50 per cent. Such concerns might mask indolence, for older students are commonly regarded as more demanding and more discriminating. But the concern is in my experience most commonly professionally reputable.

Other teaching staff attitudes, 'prejudices' in the non-pejorative sense of judgements arrived at earlier and not easily accessible to alteration, are also encountered. Most are undoubtedly conservative in the sense of favouring the existing order; this is not sufficient reason to reject them. The resistance is entwined with dislike of other changes, notably modularization, which are seen as detracting from the sustained, sequential, disciplined study of and induction into lines an academic discipline. New constitutions of subjects, whole fields like business, educational, health and administrative studies, suffer the same strictures. The part-time student, marking and following a path through a broader based degree than single honours or the broader Cambridge tripos, not completing in three years and not examined through one battery of unseens at the end of one or preferably three years, offends those for whom change means dilution and decay.

The undergraduate degree culture is evidently different for its different players: youngsters straight from school and maybe away from home for the first time; older local students caring for a family, holding down a job, conscious of being 'Rita'; and the 'long-term residents' and custodians of the university, the academic and other staff who represent its traditions and its continuities. Secretaries and porters can be powerful custodians, and the ageing profile of the AUT's membership is not irrelevant to its instinct and facility for change. Because this is a 'soft', non-quantifiable aspect of institutional change, internal culture and interpersonal tension are too easily overlooked in the calculus which this book examines.

Resources

Resources are more tangible than culture, although their separation from the subjective, from the instinctual and from self-interest is not always tidy. To the hard-pressed administrator of a hard-up institution facing a steady erosion of the unit of resource (less money per student), diversifying the student intake may appeal. An obvious example (outside the remit of this book) is overseas students, a significant factor in institutional budgets and a richer vein to work for 'outside earned income' than are, for example, most CE short courses. Overseas students mean cultural diversification in a more obvious way than do local non-traditional home students. They raise similar questions about integrated or separate provision (including residential accommodation and student support services), sometimes in more acute form.

Overseas students are a significant source of income, however their teaching is arranged. As modularization becomes normal, there are more opportunities to combine different groups and kinds of students and to achieve rationalization, economies of scale and viability for specialized courses. Part-time and other CE students using the university to meet their learning needs may require teaching outside the normal teaching day and week. Some British universities find departments spontaneously or administrations directively suggesting or requiring regular undergraduate teaching outside the 'nine to five' day, in 'unsocial hours'. Small classics courses are saved by re-scheduling to six p.m., when young full-time and older part-time degree groups can combine.

A more drastic variation is to shift courses to the weekend and to a more intensive format. Then degree and CE students sponsored by an employer and not free during the week may combine to achieve their similar yet different learning outcomes. Britain is familiar with the OU summer school, now emulated for instance in external MBA programmes. It is less familiar with the intensive summer semester in which regular full- and part-time undergraduates and CE students combine to make up viable, and sometimes for teachers quite lucrative, courses, although such teaching is done in Britain for American and increasingly for other overseas students.

Such timetabling changes open the university to a wider variety of learners, at the cost of altering its familiar ways. As formerly separate, marginal, CE and income-generating activities meld with 'the real teaching work of the university', questions about contracts and conditions of service are asked. Personal and pedagogic interests get mixed up. When the University of Warwick committed itself fully to part-time undergraduate degrees around 1986, there was bitter talk at Faculty Board about teaching in the sinister twilight hours, when decent folk were getting off home. Elsewhere, more covertly, a (female) professor is cited as protesting that it interfered with one's sex life! Conversely it is pointed out with only gentle malice that young undergraduates prefer six or seven p.m. to nine or ten a.m. for classes, late nights and late mornings being part of young student culture.

There will be payment for and income from teaching different kinds of students, and possible bounty for part-time and disadvantaged students if the access bandwagon rolls on. This apart, there are logistic arguments for recruiting and combining more diverse groups of students, and for spreading teaching through the day and the year wherever facilities are available. Payment and income for part-time students are problematic, but the official myopia which prevents resources following policies in support of part-time students is not the subject of this book.

Suffice it to say that students living at home do not require residential accommodation, or even the efforts of a housing officer to find them digs. So they have another attraction for the capital-hungry bursar lacking funds for new buildings. On the other hand their needs for student services, although usually modest, differ from the needs of young people for whom the institution is still, in part, *in loco parentis*. Counselling, study skills and careers, not to mention library services, may need to be widened and diversified. Less tangibly, shifting to the service station paradigm may imply innovation in curriculum and teaching methods. This may mean more staff development (the subject of Chapter 7), which also carries a price tag.

Pitching for pluralism

How far have British universities recognized and achieved resolution in respect of the mix and possible tension between different kinds of students? How far have they visualized and begun planning for the different teaching arrangements, and culture, which the service station model of an HEI implies? How many will try to back off as long as demand from eighteen-year-olds rises, leaving 'special education' to special institutions? How many will go for steady state and the old paradigm, leaving access via growth to others?

The positive and generous answer is that most universities are embracing optimistic pluralism. In the same breath, often on the same page, one university after another refers to its appeal to young people at school, reflected in high per-place UCCA numbers and high and rising aggregate A level scores; and to commitment to widen the social intake, attract more local students, make better allowance for disadvantaged groups. The pull of a strong collegiate teaching tradition and a gentle southern, or lively northern, city sits beside the promise to vary further the traditional curriculum, to introduce new subject constellations, new assessment methods, new partnerships with local FE colleges which will draw in more working class and other excluded older local students.

The majority of statements mention plans to strengthen academic staff development, and absence of reference to possible tension does not prove that this is not recognized. The statements are necessarily bullish, being calculated to encourage the UFC to invest in growth there rather than down the road. None the less, it seems certain that universities which adhere to their committed aims and objectives in the coming years will experience a lot more internal grinding and jarring as the nature and meaning of the new paradigm are experienced and become clearer through that experience.

A middle generation university with a distinct regional identity but strong national appeal well exemplifies the 'both barrels' approach. It claims a place among Britain's top ten in popularity, with an applications-to-place ratio of 13.7 : 1. It has no doubts about expanding student numbers while sustaining quality. Its plans include more student residences. At the same time is makes a cogent bid for expanding non-traditional entry, using its regional identity and strong FE Access links, and claims to be closely monitoring GCSE and National Curriculum developments to be responsive to the new circumstances of non-traditional young as well as older students. It offers first-year exemption through a certificate programme and is 'introducing a full unitization of its courses, a standardized degree structure and a modular degree option available to students after their first year' as well as planning to extend credit transfer. It plans a 50 per cent increase in the proportion of mature and NSE undergraduates during the planning period. It claims success for an existing two plus two scheme, promises transferable skills as well as high quality, and also promises support for quality assurance from its staff development unit.

Another university of similar age but less natural advantage makes less play of its magnetism, although claiming to draw very widely nationally, and to have a reputation for good teaching and appeal from its friendly atmosphere. It too plans to build more student residences. It sees its local market, especially for part-time students, as limited but makes strong play of access and of modularization, which was introduced in 1987 and is now being universalized. Although it has not joined CNAA CATS as such it plans to extend credit transfer on the back of full modularization. Another positive claim is for its high mature age intake (partly protected by quotas) and high NSE intake. The argument for expansion is anchored more in economies of scale than in high demand, although quality finds the usual place in the statement. Like the first example, CE in its broad sense permeates the statement very widely, giving the impression again of a university which has determined to shift to a broader-based undergraduate population within the 'new paradigm'.

Let us take one more example from the same generation of universities, also clear in its planning statement about the centrality and permeability of CE in the broad sense. Here again there are plans to add to undergraduate residential accommodation. Moreover, the greater part of the planned increase in undergraduate numbers, whether school-leavers or mature students, 'will be admitted with traditional A-levels no different in average grades than heretofore; the needs of increased numbers of non-traditionally qualified entrants are being addressed'; this will be done by a variety of means, including access and foundation courses in collaboration with FE, and rapidly expanding part-time course provision, some designed especially to meet the needs of the large local Asian community. The university 'shares the general trend towards more continuous assessment', is active in the CAT arena, and was considering [*sic*] 'the wider adoption of modular course structures'. On the one hand this statement refers to education throughout life – a sign of a paradigm shift? On the other its capital expenditure section writes in a hard-nosed way about an increased 11 per cent capacity yield by extending the teaching day by an hour: 'there is overlapping of joint undergraduate/continuing education teaching during the early evenings' – an example of the administrator's resource approach referred to earlier in this chapter.

Many in this generation of universities have moved *de facto* towards a learning centre model of a university, with CE in its broad sense strongly integrated. Some are more cautious. One writes of 'flexible curricula (modularization, common years, etc.)' and of broadening access and increasing common first-year and combined honours teaching. Modularization by 1992 should enhance flexibility and choice, permitting much more part-time study, and also remove duplication of teaching effort and create more cost-effective use of accommodation. While NSE students should increase from 12.2 to 15 per cent of undergraduates, the average A/AS level score was also to rise from 21.3 to 23.0 out of the maximum possible of 30.

Another makes no bones about its top research rating and its traditional emphasis on science and technology, nor, however, about its long tradition of service to the local community. It looks to attract more entrants from under-represented social groups, and also to respond 'by reviewing the style and structure of its teaching in order to attract students from differing educational backgrounds and to encourage more locally-based students'. It looks to greater modularization and a CAT system, and 'to establish a uniform teaching timetable based on a semester system'. Cooperation with FE features and 'in particular it will extend the range of phased degree courses for "access" students under a franchising arrangement with local colleges and institutions of further education', but it will also increase its residential accommodation. Revision of course structures will take account of an expected increase in part-time undergraduate students.

This sample is taken from the redbrick universities created later than the great Victorian civics. Although the former colleges of advanced technology display obvious differences arising from their more industrial origins and identities and their continuing sandwich provision, a quite similar overall impression derives from a scan of the plans of the new universities and of the major civics: some hedging of bets, widespread pluralism, a few cases where commitment to new structures and significant efforts to widen access are guarded, not to say slippery; but generally the addition of a latently powerful interacting set of innovations leading towards an 'NSE paradigm', while still putting up new halls of residence and predicting yet higher A level scores from a traditional clientele.

6 | Access, Quality and Success – Old and New Criteria

Access and quality are among the two most prominent policy issues in British higher education. Access emerged in the late 1980s. Quality appeared a little later, if anything still more dramatically. Here I first consider the 'access debate' and the emergent 'quality debate', then examine the connections between them, with reference mainly to continuing education. I turn next to a consideration of 'success' in HE teaching. Can a new paradigm be discerned to do with what constitutes success, and how is it measured? The chapter concludes by explaining how conscious and how salient new criteria for access, quality and success appear to be.

The access debate

The Society for Research into Higher Education made access its final annual conference theme of the 1980s. The volume for that event (Fulton 1989) is just one of many publications to appear about that time on the same theme. The RSA's involvement yielded *Aim Higher* and *More Means Different*, both subtitled 'widening access to higher education' (Ball 1989, 1990). The Training Agency contributed *Admission to Higher Education. Policy and Practice*, and BP *Increasing Participation in Higher Education* (Fulton and Ellwood 1989; Smithers and Robinson 1989).

Leslie Wagner traces government's increasing support for access both to increase the age participation rate or APR (the proportion of each age cohort entering higher education as it reaches eighteen) and to widen access to under-represented groups (Fulton 1989: Chapter 9). Wagner finds a change in climate as a result of this persisting rhetoric, making access 'central not marginal; legitimate not sinful; and internal not external to higher education' (Fulton 1989: 156). On the whole, however, public finance has not followed the rhetoric. A year later his scepticism about both Government and institutional commitment had deepened. In an article bylined 'the outlook for adults in higher education is bleak, indeed bleaker than it has been for a considerable time', he is pessimistic that student loans and a rising APR will reduce mature student demand for and entry to HE. Wagner comes squarely to the question of whether there is a genuine shift or merely temporizing during a difficult period:

> Now comes the test. Were all these conversions to the cause of access genuine in intent, or just convenient postures to tide institutions over what was expected to be a sticky period? We shall see, and I fervently hope that I am proved wrong in my suspicion that for some institutions, particularly the universities, the commitment to wider access will disappear as quickly as it arrived if 18-year-old demand stays buoyant.
>
> Wagner 1990: 94–5

Clark Brundin expressed it early in the new decade: 'The international flavour of the year in higher education is expansion. Almost no country seems happy with current participation rates' (*THES* 8 February 1991: 8). In his university the argument about widening access has been couched in terms of responsibility to the local and national community rather than space left by fewer eighteen-year-olds. Wagner's 'buoyant demand' from the young may suffice to meet the more modest targets for expansion, and so could keep most HEI departments in business. It should not prevent widening access for non-traditional older as well as young 'target groups', although the practical competition for places at the level of each admissions tutor presents a severe dilemma. Slippage between institutional policy and departmental behaviour can be substantial. The larger point, however, is the global trend towards massively expanding HE systems, and a similarly universal question about what this means for the structure and management of the system, and the roles of different HEIs within this. It is this context which gives the 'access debate' its full breadth and texture.

The fuel is not temporary demographic perturbation but the unceasing perturbation of technological innovation, socio-cultural change and the requirement for lifelong learning and adaptation. The question is not whether wider access and enhanced CE will occur, but the form these will take, the roles of different institutions and programmes within this, and the consequences to which different answers to these questions may lead. Let us now look at the yet newer 'debate' about quality, then return to access and especially to the national system for quality assurance in access which links these developments.

The quality debate

> Apart from finance, questions of 'quality' and 'accountability' in higher education are inevitably going to be principal themes in the higher education policy debate in future years.
>
> Loder 1990: xi

Loder's volume is mainly concerned with the part different quality assurance agencies and mechanisms do or might play in British HE. It first notes how highly the quality of British HE is regarded:

It is clearly dangerous to give too much weight to this kind of beauty contest [a *Liberation* survey of European HEIs] but the high proportions of British institutions mentioned in nearly all subject areas is a matter for some satisfaction and should not be forgotten when considering the self-criticism and proposals for reform in the rest of the book.

Loder 1990: 1

The high quality and high success rate of the small and elite British HE system partly explains the sudden concern with quality, hard on the heels of access. 'More means worse' is now whispered rather than shouted, but 'more means different' may sound similar to academic ears. 'More means better' is too bold to digest quickly. New-found autonomy in the public sector, the rapid expansion of the polytechnics, ambiguity over who guards quality, and the changing role and early demise of the CNAA are all factors in the new concern (Bird and Callaghan 1990; Clarke *et al.* 1991). The CVCP created an Academic Audit Unit in 1990 to monitor quality assurance mechanisms for teaching in the universities. Quality features in the UFC's first and seventh aims (access is the theme of the fourth aim). UFC Circular 39/89 inviting offers and planning statements sought a section on teaching and learning, which 'provides the opportunity to deal with the matter of academic standards and teaching quality'. Quality assurance arrangements (along with the older terms excellence and standards) naturally feature strongly in the planning statements.

In January 1991 a conference in Birmingham, 'What Is Quality in Higher Education?', attracted over two hundred participants from the HE establishment. It was addressed by chief executives from each interest and body centrally involved: PCFC and UFC, HMI, CNAA and the CVCP's AAU, as well as the management of HEIs. Significant in itself and interesting for presentations by two industrialists on total quality as a never-ending process (and for the reaction of the HE community to these two presentations), the conference was notable for the numbers it attracted. It also launched a three-year transbinary research project on quality. By then UCACE had already examined quality in CE at its 1990 annual conference, set up a working party on quality, and secured £90,000 from the UFC for a development project on quality in CE running to 1994. In the opening year of the nineties, quality as a policy agendum had well and truly arrived.

The surge in interest in quality is partly a result of the British binary system, and of the autonomy granted to the polytechnics in April 1989. Their relationship with the CNAA changed rapidly, albeit not quickly enough for some who were impatient of earlier procedures and controls. As polytechnics approximate to the universities in academic freedom, and in competing for students and status, comparisons suggest themselves between quality assurance practices developed with and through the CNAA, which are visible and transparent, and the less visible and perhaps less systematic arrangements, relying heavily on peer scrutiny and the external examiner system, of the universities. University teaching appears vulnerable on two counts: it is more costly, yet less systematic on matters of quality, than that of the polytechnics.

It is little wonder that quality features prominently in planning statements, even without the overt requirements of the UFC, which in turn looks over its shoulder at the Government.

The structure and inbuilt competitiveness of the binary system may have pushed quality up the agenda. The Jarratt Report (Jarratt 1985) attempted to improve universities' management. The battle goes on between universities and spokespersons of the Government, as institutions discover financial deficits and are pushed into staff appraisal and development. Through the AAU, the CVCP attempts to respond to and contain these pressures. A little earlier the CVCP's Staff Development and Training Unit (SDTU) was set up at Sheffield amidst scepticism about its role and viability. The DES is reportedly sceptical whether appraisal is tough enough. The AAU is described as 'cheap and cheerful' (*THES* 8 February 1991), which sounds unlikely to convince political masters about rigour.

There persists a sense of scepticism on both sides of the quality debate: those who 'know quality when we see it, but can't describe what it is'; and those who see this as a recipe for doing nothing (as was asserted at the Birmingham Quality Conference), or say in turn that 'if it can't be measured it doesn't exist' (as was also maintained at the same event). Yet quality is the flavour of the year in the early nineties, as was access at the end of the eighties, to judge by the succession of conferences, research and development projects and even full length books (Loder 1990; Berdahl *et al.* 1991). Dates of AAU visits are swapped and early horror stories do the rounds; political party statements are scanned for clues of what might follow the old CNAA and the new AAU.

This book is not about quality as such: the relative merits of total quality management and BS 5750; the fears that mechanistic measures will curdle true academic quality in the name of quality assurance and control; or, on the other hand, the completion that devious academic minds may again be turning to eloquent self-serving protectionism, guarding the unquestioned goodness of the status quo. However, the market–producer–consumer connotations which (total) quality (control) have for the academy connect this issue with our linked themes of new discourse and a paradigm shift.

A recent comparative Anglo-American study of access and quality – in a common context of resource constraint and rising managerialism – shows the parallel interplay between access and quality in these two systems, drawing out the natural connection between the two debates (Berdahl *et al.* 1991). I return now to access in British universities and its connection with quality, before asking what is looked for as success in university teaching.

Quality control in access

In the political and administrative circumstances of the early 1990s, following a decade of restricted HE expenditure by a Government inimical to public sector spending, and in a world of essentially similar trends in HE, performance measures, audit and quality control were bound to become part of the new discourse. Access means greatly increasing the size of the sector. It inevitably raises the question of whether the same standard can be attained as with a tiny, highly selected minority.

Institutions are expected to expand with relatively fewer resources, depreciating the 'unit of resource' and the staff–student ratio (SSR). Secretaries of State insist that the gold standard of the British degree must not be debased. It is not clear whether, politically speaking, more is allowed and meant to mean different. Should HEIs adapt to new kinds of students, with different learning experiences and needs? Can and will they? Does maintaining standards mean all undergraduates going through the same (kinds of) courses by the same (kinds of) means as in the past?

There is already great diversity: between an OU degree experience, reading for a degree at an Oxbridge college, and a sandwich degree partnered with industry at a technological university. Is it a matter of rate of innovation rather than diversity? These and other forms of HE can be considered 'gold standard degrees' as long as the HE establishment and the community, especially employers, have time to get used to the novelty. How fast can change be accommodated? How can it be facilitated?

Access courses as a major form of second chance education and a third route into higher education (with A levels and BTEC) raise the questions about quality discussed above. Access courses are mainly provided by FE colleges. Usually a local arrangement with one or more HEIs gave recognition – perhaps quite limited and informal, department to department at that HEI, perhaps more formal, public and generalizable through HE generally. This remains the dominant form of Access, although the range, style and format has widened. Some HEIs are themselves Access providers or co-providers. Concern about a national framework for Access courses, by 1990 numbering some 600, and about reassuring HEIs and government about their quality, led the CNAA, in partnership with CVCP and in consultation with DES and the main funding bodies, to set up the transbinary Access Courses Recognition Group. ACRG tries to combine quality assurance with 'lightness of touch'. It has created a national network of Authorised Validating Agencies (AVAs), which approve and monitor Access courses.

It is early days to judge the success of ACRG. A research project monitors its development, with formative evaluation back to ACRG (Parry and Davies 1991). ACRG is a microcosm for issues of quality and HE expansion. It was important to win the trust of the older educational establishment and of such key players as the Open University, the University of London, and the Joint Matriculation Board; but also to win over the 'access movement' – the Open Colleges and FAST.

It is a slippery tightrope. Is the 500 hours' study guideline a firm rule? If it gets interpreted rather as class contact one is back into 'time-serving', not forward to competences. How is sensible, rational, regional transbinary partnership to be encouraged? How can it be ensured that FE is in full partnership when its representation on ACRG is light? Does one trust the processed word of the submission, face to face meetings with AVA representatives, or only the inspectoral visit which ACRG avoids? How does the ACRG, in legitimating Access courses, avoid devaluing other forms of return-to-learn which can prepare for higher education? Does providing quality assurance, clearing and signposting the Access route, bar off other routes, and reduce access in the name of quality? Such are the practical considerations involved in seeking quality assurance 'on the ground': how to keep the baby clean but avoid drowning it in the bathwater.

CAT and quality

CNAA also promotes credit accumulation and transfer by means of its CAT scheme, the most salient national arrangement for promoting a common credit point tariff. The activity is replicated through local and regional CAT associations and consortia as well as tariff-rating work in different HEIs. The boundaries of CAT operations (CNAA and other) can be pushed further and further out. The OU and Scotland posed problems of equivalence. Another consortium is concerned with CAT Europe-wide, and the Commonwealth of Learning includes CAT among its worldwide concerns.

CAT and wider access to HE can be pushed further out in other ways. It can be achieved by widening admission into HEIs, but also by extending HE provision, or the recognition for academic credit of learning achieved, outside the walls of the HEIs and the rolls of the Open University. CAT spills over into the accreditation of prior experiential learning (APEL) and into employer-based and employer-provided education and training. Some is already recognized by the CNAA for undergraduate (three levels) and graduate (M level) credit points. Within the education system CNAA negotiates for common recognition or exchange of credit with other bodies, including NCVQ, professional and employer organizations. By 1991 validation and franchising arrangements (home and overseas) were also on the CNAA agenda.

Access courses are essentially egalitarian. AVAs must adopt equal opportunity intentions, and cannot grade their Access certificates. In the CAT Scheme courses are classified as earning credit points, both general and (subject-) specific, at one or another *level*. An ACRG-authorized Access certificate in effect 'matriculates' for study within HE. It also seeks to guarantee quality for and at that level, through FHE partnership and peer scrutiny.

Level and quality are different but connected. As long as the fact (technical fiction but abiding 'social fact'?) of the common standard of the British honours degree is kept as a policy imperative, quality assurance will operate within an assumption about levels. Attempts to introduce an initial two-year degree have, like the Diploma in Higher Education (Dip HE), yet to command political and academic support (Schuller 1990b; also the *Guardian* 2 July 1991).

Quality in CE

University continuing educators in Britain have become keenly interested in quality. Their American counterparts are ahead of them in developing professional modes and measures for quality control. This interest derives partly from the non-examined, non-award-bearing character of most of the work, both liberal and vocational. PICKUP is judged variable on the rare occasions when it has been assessed other than by the customers who vote with their feet and with cheque books. In April 1989 when the Responsible Body system ended, HMI ceased to inspect extramural classes. These thus lost their external quality assurance mechanism. Continuing education departments are creating different arrangements, internally and through quality circles as in Scotland, to all appearances more vigorously than are those who mainly teach undergraduates.

There are two likely reasons. First, university adult education (UAE) is historically exposed, lacking the examination system which, using external examiners, attempts national comparability of standards (on the external examiner system see Chapter 3 of Loder 1990). Secondly, in the absence of such a system it is a matter of assertion rather than proof that the work is appropriate to a university level. The Australian Federal Government decided in the 1960s to terminate support for UAE on the ground that it was 'sub-university level'. It took intensive lobbying and the personal intervention of the Prime Minister to have the decision reversed.

Where British extramural departments did certificate their courses (other than by preparing students for others' qualifications) the resulting awards lacked currency. They were not recognized even as matriculating, much less carrying standing within a degree (Duke and Marriott 1973). In the more entrepreneurial late 1980s, CE departments moved into Access apparently unhindered and unworried by its sub-degree status – qualifying, that is, for entry into the first year (level 1) of degree work. More securely, they increasingly provide and examine for certificate and diploma courses offering some advanced standing within undergraduate degrees. Appropriateness by level then seems assured, while quality can be assured within the national quality assurance framework.

Note how questions of quality and access take us to the related matter of what it is appropriate for a university to be doing. Resources are limited and there is severe competition – within teaching, between teaching and research, between subject areas, between institutions and sectors. What deserves highest priority? What is it most fitting to do, since one cannot do everything? Temptation points down the path of differentiation between institutions – an R–T–X kind of categorization. No doubt the HE system *will* move towards further differentiation in becoming unitary, but at what price and with what rigidity?

Let us turn now to the idea that indicators of success may need refreshing, and re-defining, for the system as a whole.

Learning and degrees

High demand for undergraduate places and high A level scores for those admitted were prominent among the criteria for high standards and a claim on the UFC for resources to expand in 1990. Both are visible, quantifiable and national. Less common was the proportion of good (first and upper second class) honours degrees. This may be less satisfactory. Why does one institution award proportionately more firsts than another, and why is there at times such wide variation between departments within the one institution? This measure is output-related, as is employability – an increasingly important indicator – whereas A levels are an input measure. Like demand per place, they measure popularity, but only indirectly, perhaps, excellence. Selectivity ratings give a public, partly quantified measure of the research output of each department or cost centre, which now translates into institutional income.

These measures have little to do with the quality of what is done, insofar as this is about the *processes* of production, whether the product be machine tools, biscuits or learning. If success is about institutional standing, intake measures serve well enough. If it is about something else – contribution to national human resource development, to economic regeneration or implementing equal opportunity – other measures must be employed. We are as concerned here with the criteria whereby universities reckon success as with the impact of quality upon access. Identifying a new paradigm from this perspective means asking how success is valued and measured, not just whether concerns about quality inhibit the rapid and effective development of access.

Use of the new discourse introduced in Chapter 2 may betray a shift in thought. Modularization and credit-rating allow new measures of success. Some institutions refer explicitly to equal opportunity in their planning statements, with regard to admissions as well as management practices. Others (same purposes, different words) aspire to widen and diversify their intake of undergraduates to include larger numbers from under-represented socio-economic and ethnic groups. Others seek more students from the locality, even using the word commuters. Supply may create demand, or perhaps demand is already partly being met. Here are the bones of quite new PMs that could readily be calibrated to measure the success of HEIs. They could be direct PMs within the access paradigm, distinct from those quality considerations which serve as surrogates rather than direct measures: staff development and appraisal, student support services, curriculum review and monitoring procedures.

Such a shift means using social as well as purely academic intake (or input) measures. The shift from academic to social offends some who may overlook the fact that selective intake is not socially and politically neutral: A level scores favour the socially privileged, notably from the private school sector, and confuse past attainment with future potential, as well as excluding notions of need. A further step would relate intake attainment levels to final results; in other words it would measure value added or 'talent development' (Berdahl *et al.* 1991).

The change in funding from UGC to UFC, like earlier changes in the funding of adult education while it was still under the DES, is a shift from funding the infrastructure (staff costs, block grant) to funding the product or output. Universities offer to educate so many degree-getting students in different subject areas, and to produce so many FTEs of liberal adult education within their agreed geographical region, in return for an agreed price per product. With regard to liberal adult education the UFC contracts universities to undertake different amounts of different categories of work, paying more for some than others: Access, award-bearing, disadvantaged and other high cost provision. Once this principle is established there is no technical reason why it could not be extended to all teaching. Certain categories of students as well as subjects could be differentially rewarded: affirmative action could apply thus, as it does already to high-value and high- or low-cost subjects.

Let us pause to note an ambiguity and an opportunity. The ambiguity concerns product and process. UFC pays to have students taught subjects, not directly ('payment by results') for output. Universities measure success by output – number and class of degrees. The UFC currency presents an opportunity, along with modularization, for universities more fully to recognize and reward the teaching process via completed modules of study. Most do resource (i.e. reward) departments for the teaching done and not for the degrees at the end. It is a short technical step (but a larger paradigm leap) to abandon the idea of degrees – terminal, the educated person finished with learning – and to treat study and attainment only by accumulated credit in a lifelong record of achievement. Recurrent education might then have arrived.

In practice there has been little movement in shifting the meaning of success. Two-year degrees look no more marketable than the Dip HE, although the campaign gathers energy. Disaggregating the final honours degree as *the* measure of individual (and institutional) attainment looks no more promising. The annual 'terminal' graduation ceremony (an unwitting statement against lifelong recurrent education) will probably long remain with us – graduation of the 'class of '79' into the 'real world' outside!

The Vice-Chancellor of Warwick University, reflecting on his Californian roots, is on record as saying that British HE has too high a success rate. The best is the enemy of the good. Selection is so severe, expectation of success so high, that the system wants only safe and certain graduaters. In the United States students who leave the system after a year or two of full-time study or, very likely, its part-time or interrupted equivalent, use such credit accumulated in one or more institutions as part of their curriculum vitae and a basis for advancement. Jokes about BA Oxford (failed) make the point: normally there is completion or nothing, but overcome by Oxford's massive prestige! Normally one covers up rather than admits to going to university unless there is a degree to show for it. The learning and education completed are nothing; the final degree is everything.

Modularization or unitization of study could change all this if institutions would publicly measure educational effort in terms of separate courses, rather than degrees completed. A modular structure requires this measurement of effort and allocation of resources anyway. New degree structures tend to build in 'terminal points', or bus stops, along the way. Stopping points to satisfy different needs use the familiar certificate–diploma–degree triarchy at both undergraduate and graduate levels. Stopping off qualifications are still seen mainly as falling short; they lack appeal as destinations in their own right.

Within the national culture (as within a profession or institution) a new paradigm could form in the arms of the old, then step full-grown into life. So far, however, the democratizing potential of modularization and CAT in universities has been obscured by the focus on flexibility and economies of provision and scale – or, put more negatively, the fragmentation of formerly coherent curricula into pick'n'mix packages.

Quality with expansion

Whatever may be shaping beneath, little appears to have changed on the surface. We find little overt tension between the established residential finishing school and the new access paradigm. Among the planning statements for 1991–5 the assumption is coexistence of old and new in the plural university, with perhaps just one exception.

Many institutions claim high quality for their teaching via the twin intake criteria: demand for places and aggregate A level scores of those accepted. Some predict still higher scores on these two measures. Many also promise to admit more non-traditional or NSL students: adult and young students from under-represented socio-economic and ethnic groups. Many add a general assurance that this will not diminish quality or standards. All refer to measures whereby teaching quality will be sustained and curricula renewed. The non-traditional intake is usually specified as local or regional. Equal opportunity is mentioned by name occasionally. Some institutions commit themselves to increasing the number or proportion of mature age students. Others prefer generalizations.

A number of universities do refer in the access context to efforts to adapt curriculum and admission arrangements to take account of new curricula and examinations, particularly the National Curriculum but also in some cases the courses and examinations found in FE and more vocational secondary schools. A few universities describe the development of non-traditional degree structures, and especially of partnerships with further education, which are intended to widen access.

What about partnerships? What does the trend towards substantial and plural links between HEIs and FE colleges signify? If quality can be secured, this might prove a rapid bypass route to mass higher education. 'Two plus two' degrees expand access and HE by sharing the work with FE colleges. Franchising out or sub-contracting the first year of the degree programme to FE colleges lends itself naturally to large areas with a dispersed population such as north-west and south-west England, but is not restricted to such locations. Validation of courses allows students who may never visit the university to obtain its degree or diploma. Familiarity with the work of CNAA as a national validating body may obscure the importance of this growing practice as a mode of enlarging the HE system. One university with 12,000 students can change that number to 20,000 at the stroke of a pen by adding those on validated courses also working towards its degrees.

CNAA validates access courses which foster FE–HE partnerships through the AVAs, and is extending CAT into many settings beyond the HEIs. Existing universities, which have been growing more slowly than the polytechnics, may not grow very much more. The character of British universities might in one sense change and evolve only modestly. Yet university numbers could greatly expand through various forms of outreach, franchising and validation, quite apart from the re-naming of polytechnics as universities. Britain has a reputation for pragmatism and gradualism. Is this particular genius again on display? Will a new paradigm both emerge and not emerge? 'Success' then means changing while not changing!

I return to this theme in Chapter 8 in considering the increasingly permeable boundaries and open membership of most universities.

The new universities

The eight greenfield universities created in the 1960s might be expected to value innovation and new measures of success, though they were created with the Oxbridge residential model in mind and influenced by Oxbridge staffing. It has been remarked how conservative the Robbins reforms really were, and how similar *all* UK HEIs actually are one to another, by international comparison.

All their plans include sustaining and enhancing efforts to widen access. One is restricted by its catchment area. Another, with a large hinterland, makes much of its Open College network and arrangements with the OU. In most cases access features as a significant and major element. On the other hand six of the eight universities mention high demand for places through the UCCA system. Ratios of the order of 20 : 1 stress how demand has risen in recent years.

Most have always exercised discretion and flexibility in their admissions. A level scores are not an over-riding preoccupation. Only one mentions aggregate scores as evidence of high standards. It is the least whole-hearted in the broad access field (including part-time degree), also emphasizing its very low wastage or drop-out rate. A 'no-risk' preoccupation is a barrier to widening access. Yet even this university boasts high mature age numbers in some departments, welcomes the changes in school curriculum, accepts a wide variety of 'unconventional' qualifications and has no formal matriculation requirement. Five of the eight similarly mention school-level changes as being in line with the university's existing practices.

A majority claims high proportions of mature age (twenty-one plus on entry) or non-traditional admissions. One finds this incompatible with competing for high A level scores; for another it does not depress completion and quality of degrees. One only cites its enhanced proportion of good honours degrees over recent years. All set out quality assurance and curriculum review procedures to sustain and extend the interdisciplinarity, flexibility and choice that are a group hallmark.

There are few specific targets for NSEs during the planning period, but general commitment to continue or increase above-average proportions: 'continue to admit a high proportion of mature students' (currently 17 per cent compared with 11.5 per cent nationally); 'continue the practice which is currently 26 per cent, over double the national average'; (currently 28 per cent of undergraduates are aged over 21 on entry); 'further improve on the present 20 per cent mature intake and 27 per cent admitted other than on A and AS levels'. Several universities explain their special regional responsibility to widen access, more especially for social classes III to V. One notes its above average intake from these classes, referring to 'various inner city initiatives' and claiming high value added – a term little used in any of the statements. Another records an increase in local demand, especially from mature age applicants, and refers to inner city plans and to aspirations to increase the intake from social classes III to V.

Already high mature age and non-traditional intakes may inhibit these universities from setting specific targets, although most pledge further increases. Numbers where specified are for part-time students but even here most are non-specific or evasive, perhaps because greenfield sites do not lend themselves so easily to local part-time attendance. One university gives precise targets for part-time and two plus two students under a new scheme to be launched with local FE colleges during the planning period. This is one of five new universities to refer to validation of courses (some refer only to validation of Access courses). New institutions are disadvantaged in the validation stakes by their newness, except in a new field like Access; but references to local association or collaboration suggest that the principle of enhanced access through inter-institutional cooperation is adopted so far as is practicable.

Other signs of new thinking go beyond the curriculum review and flexibility shared by all these institutions but stop short of a new mode such as 'two plus two'. One refers to plans for accelerated entry to the second year of undergraduate degrees 'for particularly well-qualified [mature age] candidates, including those possessing appropriate Open University credits'. The university planning 'two plus two' also gives advanced standing for certificated courses taken through its adult education programme. Another has under consideration changing the measures rather than just accelerating the progression towards existing ones: 'the certification of periods of study amounting to less than the full honours degree courses is under consideration' – this is an understandably guarded statement, given the persisting national preoccupation with three-year full-time or equivalent degrees and the resistance to 'dilution'.

The stars were in the same firmament when all these universities were born. Each values flexibility and interdisciplinarity although the meaning varies from place to place. They are quite open to new measures of success, despite traditional influences in their formative years. Differences of style and assertiveness reflect differences of leadership. Geography also plays a part. Warwick, now by far the largest, also has the strongest industrial base and is in this sense more similar to a civic university. Although all are greenfield, the actual location affects the sense of opportunity as far as access is concerned.

The English civics

A second sample of universities is the seven large civics founded in the nineteenth century and located in big industrial cities. Superficially there are differences of tone in the way they present themselves: boldly innovative and bullish; more cautiously hedging bets. More striking, however, are two things: the confident duality whereby what in this book are called old and new paradigms are reflected or espoused; and the prominence with which different elements indicative of the newer paradigm repeatedly feature.

Is it surprising that this generation of universities should mostly appear to embrace change as well as continuity? A cynical response would be 'No, since more than half have been named as being in financial trouble, and getting out of trouble means toeing the government line.' Another reaction might be: 'Yes, amazing. They are chronically arthritic in terms of committee non-decision-making structures. Jarratt-led changes are only skin-deep. Anyway, saying and delivering are not the same thing.' A more charitable, but possibly also more accurate answer might be: 'Not really. These institutions were founded by and on local communities. They are in a sense merely rediscovering their roots as the pendulum between internationalism and regionalism re-adjusts. And anyway, they are mostly led by open-minded and public-spirited people for whom national needs and institutional survival are not in conflict.'

Be that as it may, six of the seven boldly include widening access at the heart of their mission, aims and objectives. At the same time all assert the high demand for their places through UCCA. The majority also quote the high A level scores of those they accept. At one extreme the university's A level scores and applicants per place are graphed against national averages for each subject group. Another settles for a parenthetical mention in its opening paragraph:

> the very considerable number of applications to the University (eleven times over subscribed with an average A-level entry of 23 points on a 30 point scale) supports the view that our educational enterprise is in high demand.

A third claims an average A level score (October 1989) of 23.2, and 1990 applications at 15.4 per place:

> the University has not been outside the top three in terms of gross applications through UCCA since the early 1970s . . . and the University is still increasing its proportional share of national applications.

Another claims to be in the top three by UCCA applications, and a fifth (supported by a chart) notes that more than one in every seven applicants list it on their UCCA forms. None is worried about not attracting enough highly qualified eighteen-year-olds despite the demographics. At least five have plans to increase residential accommodation during the planning period. We are not looking, in this the English university heartland, at deserting the finishing school paradigm.

What we do see is clear and sometimes quantified intentions to recruit significantly more non-traditional students. Some refer in so many words to equal opportunity. More specify their intentions for under-represented groups. Four at least refer to Afro-Caribbean or more generally to under-represented ethnic minorities, and to inner city projects intended to enhance intake from these communities. All specify mature age students and some mention women. Five at least mention changes in the school curriculum, which can affect new as well as traditional groups.

Each university (and this applies to all in the UK system) gives firm assurances about its quality assurance and review procedures, as one might expect. There is no hint of anxiety that 'more means worse' in any of the plans to expand and to diversify more into non-traditional areas of recruitment. In a positive vein, two universities refer to relevant staff development work:

> There are already substantial numbers of mature and 'non traditional' students in many Departments. Thus, discriminating experience of the new issues and dimensions that mature students present to teachers and tutors has been accumulated. Through its staff development programme the University is providing increasing support and recognition for the wider acquisition by staff of the necessary skills and techniques to respond to wider access and to changes in secondary level curricula.

And in the second instance:

> A study skills group is in operation and staff development programmes will include, for example, training for academic staff on the particular needs of mature and part-time students and those from non-traditional academic backgrounds.

One way and another these civic universities now see themselves as attracting more local students as undergraduates as well as to graduate programmes and short courses. This will tend to be in a part-time mode, although wider access encompasses full-time study if financial circumstances and support systems will allow. Some are explicit about local catchment;

others leave it implicit. Some set targets, absolute or as a proportion of total intake for non-traditional, mature age or part-time undergraduate admission. One notes that

> during the period to 1994/95 it is possible that the implementation of the Government's top-up loans policy will result in greater pressure on students and their families to economise and a consequent increase in local students commuting to the university from home. Such a develop-ment would of course strengthen the recruitment of the big civic universities .... Nevertheless we believe that any change in the propor-tion of students both able and willing to commute to the university will not be significant until at least the middle of the decade, and for that reason plan to build more residential accommodation.

Conversely the Director of Brighton Polytechnic explained to the 1991 annual conference of UCACE that student loans 'cement the three year full-time model' by favouring the socially and financially advantaged.

More equivocal still is the introductory observation that 'it is by pursuing its aim of academic excellence that the University can best play its part in the local community from which it sprang, and on the national and world stage'. Even this university is also explicit about equal opportunity in its recruitment and in including the local area, and mature students, as well as 'candidates of all social and ethnic backgrounds'.

Another sees dual development as follows:

> The University will be increasing its stock of student accommodation not least for students with families; it expects the changes which are likely in the funding of UK undergraduates to lead at the margins to a higher percentage living at home – its location at the centre of a conurbation makes it well placed to respond to any such trend – but the recent changes in the regulations relating to students and housing bene-fits are likely to increase demand for residential places.

'At the margins' is reassuring. Note, however, that housing for families here sits in the access rather than the finishing school paradigm!

Access is permeating thinking about recruitment and institutional be-haviour. For one civic university

> its Access programme recognises wider responsibilities to the commun-ity. The admission of expanded cohorts of students with a wider range of backgrounds, qualifications and experience will provide a broad cultural, social and educational environment for the benefit of all students .... Within the University, Departments and Faculties have reviewed their admissions processes to produce statements of the prior skills, learning and experience required. These statements set out a framework for the recognition not only of academic, professional and vocational qualifications but also of prior experiential learning .... The recruitment of part-time undergraduates is being encouraged .... A full

examination of the availability and adequacy of academic and other
services is being undertaken to ensure that they meet the needs of all
students, particularly mature students and those studying part-time and
evening . . . . The provision of further child-care facilities has recently
been agreed.

At another

widening access to the University is intended to ensure that all potential candidates, irrespective of their background, have an equal opportunity to apply to and benefit from its courses. Specific policies to
achieve this widening of access are:
- a flexible approach to non-standard qualifications and a recognition of the experience offered by mature students lacking formal
  qualifications . . .
- further development of part-time degree courses . . .
- an equal opportunities policy in respect of sex, age, and ethnic
  origin . . .
- a positive approach to students with disabilities
- further development of outreach courses, in which students are taught
  in local colleges; these are free-standing sub-degree level courses, Dip
  HEs, and parts of degree courses
- the appointment of a Mature Students' Adviser to give advice to
  potential mature students before application and to departments
  seeking to admit such students
- the maintenance of part-time and self-financed fees at affordable
  levels
- the Mature Access Programme . . . which prepares students with
  non-standard academic backgrounds for degree-level work in a wide
  variety of disciplines.

So the implications of access have been followed through in some institutional thinking, beyond diversification of the student body: non-traditional recruitment is planned in addition to, not in place of, the more familiar intake.
Not all universities set numbers or proportions of mature age or NSE
students. Some, pointing out how high these proportions already are, will
still continue to develop this side of their work. The university quoted above
records that its intake aged twenty-one plus has risen to 17 per cent from
9 per cent five years earlier, with 21 per cent of the intake offering qualifications other than A levels. At another civic, 'part-time students will be
increased in accordance with market demand'. In FTE terms access to
part-time courses, 'particularly for mature students, ethnic minorities,
women and the unemployed . . . currently comprises 4 per cent of all registered undergraduates but the number of part-time undergraduates is set to
rise at a faster rate than the number of full-time students'. Another civic
plans to increase part-time undergraduate numbers by 68 per cent (com-

pared with 17.3 per cent overall), and another from 530 to 900 FTEs (i.e. at least 60 per cent), while doubling NSE numbers.

Finally, several of the large civic universities describe changes and developments which will diversify modes of provision and accreditation in support of access. If successful and more numerous, these could quite rapidly break the mould of the three-year residential honours gold standard degree in favour of a more plural pattern. Single honours would doubtless still predominate but with less devaluation of other forms.

One university has set up an office for part-time education and is modularizing its programmes, which it sees as 'crucial to widening access'. It has also 'begun a dialogue with FE Colleges in the region, and plans to extend this to schools, especially inner city schools and those with substantial populations of ethnic minorities where access to HE is currently poor'. It also validates degrees in its affiliated colleges, claiming to be second only to the CNAA in this respect. Another university prefers for part-time degrees the term 'degrees by extended study', normalizing such study rather than having it ghettoized as possibly inferior. A third predicts far-reaching implications of Access:

> these include changes to course structures, to the pattern of awards, and the mode and time of attendance. The University plans to adapt courses and course structures to fit the changing applicant profile rather than applicants being selected to fit existing provisions.

A fourth civic university aims to 'develop within its extra-mural region ladders of access to award-bearing courses through systems of credit accumulation'. Its statement integrates access purposes within the different sections for each of its academic areas. It plans a range of new four-year degrees to recruit into science and technology, with a conversion element in the first year. 'A number of companies are interested in upgrading the qualifications of their BTEC employees and the University is examining the improvement of access for such students through the introduction of appropriate part-time courses.' 'Partnership', a current keyword here applied to industry and not just to other FHEIs, is seen as the way to a new form of access.

Another civic university had 989 mature age undergraduate FTEs in 1989–90, had undertaken market research, and

> plans are now well advanced for three-year part-time general degree programmes taught largely by staff in [Continuing Education] to be under the academic control of our . . . Faculties. The intention is that students would be eligible for an Honours degree after three years equivalent full-time study but would also be eligible for intermediate qualifications after one or two years equivalent full-time study if they terminated their registration at that point.

The same university plans to promote access into engineering for women and those without traditional entry qualifications through links with local FE Colleges in the provision of access and subcontracted first year courses, reviewing entrance requirements and course content and initiatives aimed at potential female students.

Here, as in an increasing number of other universities, among which Salford was probably the first, partnership with FE is seen as one mode of enhancing local access, especially for non-traditional students.

This quick tour shows that civic universities generally hope to widen 'non-traditional' access while increasing numbers of school-leavers at a more modest pace. One of their number describes 'in the context of its planned growth and the need to ensure efficiency, . . . a major curriculum development exercise' to include:

a full evaluation of all courses in terms of student contact hours, to ensure maximisation of time available for private study by students, consistent with the maintenance of academic standards; the use of all available teaching weeks for the development of more student-centred learning strategies, including individual and group project work and placements; this will be aided by the Enterprise in Higher Education and Personal Skills Units.

Space precludes a full account of the access plans of all British universities, and of their reconciliation with plans to continue as successful 'finishing schools'. The great civic universities were chosen because they are seen as central to the UK university system, and because they might be thought less willing or less able to change than the newer universities. On the other hand there may appear to be less need for change among technological universities with their industrial bases, or among the Scottish universities with their wider access and local service traditions. The civics have special significance for the evolution of the system as a whole.

In studying the civics I have briefly recalled themes from earlier chapters: the finishing school–service station mix; the possibility of a new sense of mission; the incursion of new discourse to help explain, and new curricula, accreditation and partnerships to help give effect to, wider objectives.

Managing more with less

Efficiency is sought to accompany growth. There is a note of realism in what we have been reading, as universities follow along behind the polytechnics in trying to teach more students to a continuing high standard with steadily fewer resources relative to student numbers. HE is a very labour-intensive industry, unacceptably so to any government trying to contain expenditure and expand participation. Necessity may prove the mother of invention, and a long-awaited invention at that. Can the various stratagems for encouraging self-directed and group learning be brought together? Can they be built into a viable system which provides teaching support to the increasing number of students coming into HE? Will this enable students to become more confident in managing their own learning, and so better equipped to continue learning, and to use recurrent education opportunities, throughout life as the need arises?

Learning new teaching strategies and roles is not easy. This is one reason why many universities are planning more substantial programmes of staff development, the subject of the next chapter.

7 | Staff Development and Organizational Learning

Staff development is another name for the continuing education that an organization arranges for its own members. Industry has tended to use the word training. Training officers usually have low status. The posts are stepping stones to other careers, not a distinct career path; or a parking place for some who will advance no further. Training budgets are quickly cut in a recession. Training has thus shared with continuing education the problem of marginality in the education system. The shift of language towards investment in human resources, or human resource development (HRD), heralds a re-definition of the place of 'training' in companies' strategic and business planning.

That the status and national perception of training may be a severe problem and a cause of poor national economic performance was argued time and again through the 1980s (see, for instance, Cassels 1990). Yet the theme runs back through the decades. It was a preoccupying British concern for much of the later nineteenth century (Roderick and Stephens 1984). Training and Enterprise Councils are the means whereby the Government now seeks employers' commitment to training the workforce. British enterprises are said to be more adept at poaching trained personnel than at investing in and upskilling their own. Unflattering comparison is made with Japanese companies, which are said to take responsibility for their employees in educational and other senses from recruitment to retirement. Certainly Chinese enterprises in the early eighties showed much greater company commitment and investment, relatively speaking, than is part of the UK culture (Hunter and Keehn 1985).

So 'poverty of aspiration' in terms of training or HRD is a feature of British corporate life, as of society at large in respect of post-compulsory education. The same quite small number of large and more enlightened companies feature time and again when education and industry are brought together. Neither the majority of employers nor the majority of employees take continuing education and training very seriously. Are universities, those highly prestigious corporations at the pinnacle of the massive education industry, very different?

Staff development in universities

Innocently the expectation might be positive. Education along with knowledge creation is the business of universities. Surely they take seriously the education of their own staff – the more so as HE presses its educational services on others, encouraging them to look to HEIs for workforce continuing education. Yet staff development, deliberately provided as such – the continuing education of the institution's own employees – is not a strong feature of universities' behaviour. As we shall see in a moment, however, the situation is changing.

The word faculty, referring to academic staff, provides a clue. Like the term collegiate, used in contrast to managerial, it refers to the key members of the institution – the traditionally tenured academic staff pursuing scholarship and seen, and seeing themselves, less as employees than as a kind of college or fraternity of individual scholars and professionals freely associating for the advancement of knowledge and the expression of academic autonomy. Such a community may feel ill at ease with the notion of being 'human resources' to be 'developed' in the interests of the institution. The identity and first loyalty of most scholars is with their discipline; its international community is their primary reference point. I have called the university a 'non-organization'. Staff development gets close to being intrusive and offensive. Study leave is the acceptable form of academic staff development. It is still highly individualistic in the way it is seen, defined and used.

Hence there is a paradox. Universities depend for their existence on a belief and faith in higher education. Increasingly they have to promote themselves and their educational wares: to school students, parents, employers and the broader community. Yet in terms of the organized continuing education of their own members, and especially of the more senior, that is the academic, members of the community, their record has been very poor. In place of belief and faith reside scepticism. Universities have relied rather on creating and sustaining a rich learning environment in which their scholar-teacher-researchers, as well as their students, it is hoped, can thrive, learn and grow. Just as staff development events may be felt to be intrusive, even insulting, so too has accountability for performance featured very little: professionalism and self-motivation, together with the more tangible career rewards that may follow published research, have been relied upon to make the institution productive.

All this is changing rapidly. The Government insists on appraisal of academic staff. It insists too that part of the funds for academic salaries be used in a discretionary way to reward high performance. It subjects university research to judgement via 'selectivity' and has put quality assurance in teaching on the agenda of universities. The CVCP responded by promoting staff development in the universities through its Staff Development and Training Unit in Sheffield, then set up the Academic Audit Unit in Birmingham. Staff development thus appeared among a clutch of institutional innovations thrust upon the universities and mediated through CVCP.

The 1990 planning statements provide a snapshot of how far universities were then willing to commit themselves to staff development. Indirectly the statements also convey a sense of how seriously universities were prepared to take it: not just by explicit mention in the section on staffing, but also by the content and flavour of such reference, and by whether there is reference to staff development elsewhere. This may suggest permeation rather than tokenism.

The new commitment to staff development

The UFC Aims make no explicit reference to staff development; nor did Circular 39/89 require information on the subject. The section on teaching and learning, however, suggests that 'it may be appropriate to bring in material on topics in para 23, for example on staff development and appraisal.' Paragraph 23 appears in Part Three of Annex C: 'matters which the university *may* [emphasis added] wish to include in the statement'. Among staffing policies in this part appear 'policies and arrangements for staff development and appraisal' and 'specific training policies for particular categories of staff'.

The UFC thus obliged us by setting the universities some 'optional homework'. Each was left to decide whether the subject was worth addressing. Let us now examine this 'homework' and see how, as a class, the universities performed. After that we can return to some wider questions about staff development, and what this may tell us about universities as 'adaptive learning organizations'.

Overall, universities came out much more strongly for staff development than even bold speculation in the mid-1980s might have allowed. Sixty-three planning statements were scanned and classified, according to what they said about institutions' performance and plans for staff development, into four groups: major, moderate or minor commitment to and featuring of staff development, and absence of any mention. Of the sixty-three planning statements, forty-one scored as major, thirteen as moderate and six as minor. Only three made no mention of the subject at all (see Table 7.1).

This seems to signify a remarkable turn-around from what appeared in the mid-eighties as a trend away from even the modest effort made at that time. Only a few universities then supported even the smallest of staff development units. Returning from Australia in 1985, I left a system in which every university had some such unit, under one or another of a plethora of different names but generally of adequate size to carry out the tasks of arranging programmes of induction, development and applied research mostly to do with teaching methods and the appraisal and assessment of teaching and learning. The Australian university staff development units suffered from the financial constraints of the eighties, but the culture and prospects looked far more bleak in the UK, with the exception of a very few universities like

Loughborough and Sheffield which supported vigorous units against the trend.

One can make too much of what is said in planning statements. They may be taken with a pinch of salt, but should not on the other hand be too heavily discounted, given the UFC readership. The broad categories of universities display some differences. Both the Scottish universities and the English technological universities show up strongly: six of each with major and two with moderate commitment. The London and Welsh colleges appear less wholehearted. Some make only minor mention, and one no mention at all. Some common circumstance in these two federal systems may have slowed down the shift. By contrast the civic and redbrick universities without exception score well, but the plateglass universities spread more evenly across the chart (Table 7.1).

More revealing than rank mention are the ways in which staff development is presented. Some make a direct link with quality assurance in teaching, and a few with research. Appraisal of academic staff features generally, and there is frequently a direct link made between this and staff development. Two institutions stand out exceptionally as addressing appraisal or academic audit, but making no mention of staff development. Many universities address the subject of staff recruitment and retention, as they were invited but not required to do; few make any link with staff and career development as a factor assisting retention. In this beneficial sense in which 'Japanization' is entering British management thinking, there is little sign of it penetrating the HE industry.

Different categories of staff – academic-related, technical and clerical, as well as academic – are often mentioned, and some universities have created or are in the process of setting up staff development units with an all-encompassing brief. Elsewhere academic staff development is the responsibility of one committee and perhaps officer or unit, while the development or training of other staff is handled, insofar as it is deliberately addressed, through another channel. Some state that such responsibilities are devolved (or left?) to departments, areas or cost centres. Then there is no central information, much less direction, for what is being done.

Many of the forty-one 'major' entries in Table 7.1 are bold and 'upfront'. Some literally feature up front, with a mention in the opening paragraphs and supporting detail towards the end. At the same time a striking feature, bearing witness to the remarkable shift since the mid-1980s, is the recency of the whole development, with occasional exceptions. Dates for the creation or revamping of units, for the appointment of new staff development officers, are cited: 1987, 1988, 1989, 1990. Others foreshadow structures and appointments over the next one to two years.

Will universities come to see the staff development function, and staff development units, as a necessary and permanent part of the organization's activity and infrastructure? Or is it a seven-day wonder, coming and going as fashion, or the attention of the Government and UFC, shifts to a new area, technique or tool to increase quality, efficiency and output? Staff develop-

Table 7.1 Reference to staff development in planning statements

	Major	*Moderate*	*Minor*	*No mention*
'Plateglass' or 'greenfields'	2	3	1	1
Civics and redbricks	14	–	–	–
Scottish	6	2	–	–
Technological	6	2	–	–
Welsh and London colleges	6	6	5	1
Other	7	–	–	1
Total	41	13	6	3

ment faces a long haul to become well regarded and highly valued, given the individualistic, discipline-oriented academic culture. The road will be still rockier if it is seen as a reluctant response to government pressure and CVCP pleading.

The link with appraisal may prove still more difficult. Staff development that is seen as remedial and punitive will carry a weighty stigma. Staff development that is restricted to learning how to teach may also suffer, to the extent that teaching is seen as the routine chore getting between the lecturer and the research and publication which lead to promotion. Can staff development be associated with high quality professional performance resulting in career advancement? The circle, or spiral, connecting it with appraisal, performance, audit, recognition and promotion could be vicious or beneficial. Which way the energy flows will partly determine the future health of the institutions. In a university where morale is high and leadership strong, new 'events' and interventions, such as appraisal, staff development, quality assurance, even merit payments, can feed into a positive cycle of energy mobilization and growth. In short, staff development cannot be studied, much less managed, in a vacuum.

Plans and resources for staff development

With these qualifications in mind let us look more closely at what is said about staff development.

One prestigious collegiate institution adopted a policy to identify and meet training needs for academic and managerial skills in 1986. A staff development officer (SDO) was appointed, and a comprehensive and well attended training programme introduced. The work is being extended, assisted by the appointment of a full-time SDO part-funded (presumably via EHE) by the

Training Agency. Technical and secretarial staff are mentioned, as are both internal and external courses to re-skill, following re-deployment.

In an ancient collegiate institution 'training and staff development are organised separately for academic staff, administrative staff, and assistant staff'. Examples are given and the budget for staff development is referred to. 'The new appraisal scheme for assistant staff is expected to lead to a significant increase in staff development programmes.'

Among Scottish universities, one (defined in Table 7.1 as 'moderate commitment') reports: 'our Staff Development and Appraisal Scheme came into full operation in the current session and now applies to all members of the academic and academic-related staff'. Training provision is mainly for technical, clerical and academic-related staff: 'the University Teaching Centre provides training for academic staff in teaching and assessment, particularly in early career'. Another sets out the 'five main parts' of its 'large-scale staff development programme'. The fifth part is meeting needs and requests for individual support 'emerging from the Personal Development Plans which are an important feature of the Staff Development and Appraisal Scheme'.

At a third Scottish university 'staff development is the prime emphasis of our staff appraisal scheme'. Several Scottish universities refer to collaboration with other universities in that country as well as to internal programmes. There is reference to a staff development committee and (in this small university) a part-time SDO. Early plans include establishing a staff development office as a focal point and resource centre for all staff training matters.

In another Scottish university 'the Staff Development Service is responsible for the implementation and support of the appraisal system'. The service is expanding with TA funding via EHE. Training policies are described; the level of training is increasing 'and with the formalisation of staff appraisal and development the demand is expected to grow rapidly'. Here 'training expenditure from departmental budgets and in-house provision are not separately identified'. Another refers to the appraisal scheme, now in its first year, and the appointment of a part-time SDO: 'but there remains a problem of freeing up enough resources to meet the perceived development needs'.

Two other Scottish universities refer more broadly to objectives and functions. One

> is committed to training and staff development for all groups of staff, and staff appraisal must lead to ever-increasing demands for training to be provided. We do not believe in training for training's sake, but in relation to the institution's goals and departmental needs and their achievement. An advisory structure to guide and advise the work of the recently appointed Training and Staff Development Officer (whose remit covers all staff) is being developed.

The other emphasizes its collaboration with other Scottish universities, and the extension of its staff development programme to support all staff groups.

It had in the past year, in addition to funds in support of institutional development, spent £35,000 on training

> specifically requested by employees. This sum has been used in a conscious effort to develop a culture within the University which will guarantee the success of the next planned phase of staff development policy. This will be concerned with the forging of closer links between individual demands and institutional objectives.

Some of those cited so far identified sums of money set aside for training. Others stated that it was not separately identifiable. One refers to an annual budget of £27,000 for graduate staff training and a separate staff office budget of £36,000, levels of expenditure which will at least be maintained, but are indeed very modest. One Scottish university plans to expand its staff development budget by approximately 100 per cent, without specifying what it is. Another refers simply to 'substantial resources'.

South of the border, one specialized institution intends by contrast 'to move to an allocation of 2.5 per cent of the academic salary bill to a Staff Development Fund', with the focus on rewarding and further enhancing good research performance. Another claims an all-encompassing policy. It has had a full-time training officer for some years for its non-academic staff, as well as two other members more recently appointed to make up a staff development team of three sharing clerical and administrative support. Appraisal has been introduced and woven in as part of career development policies. By 1994 a substantial increase in funding is envisaged for training and staff development, from a current budget base of £160,000.

Among the London colleges one had a half-time training officer for co-ordination, and a 1989–90 budget of £20,000 for training. Another had recently appointed a part-time academic staff development coordinator and a full-time training officer for non teaching staff. Resources for training of all staff groups have been 'significantly increased'. Another appointed a personal development coordinator in 1990 who is initiating a new training programme; and another is making efforts 'to provide an annual increase in the Training Budget over the next five years to bring it to a more realistic level'.

The London statements are mostly brief and non-specific, as are those of Welsh colleges. One of the latter has appointed a part-time SDO with an annual budget of £20,000. Another promises 'a much more pro-active role' in future for the academic staff training and development committee; the appointment of an STD officer was under consideration. Another Welsh college has a part-time academic adviser for development and training. It refers unspecifically to additional resources invested in this area from 1990, 'including the forthcoming appointment of a Staff Development Officer' in the personnel office. The impression given by the two federal systems is of a slightly late and uncertain start, but increasing recognition that staff development must be taken more seriously, and paid for.

The English universities of the 1960s are also somewhat muted in their commitment to staff development. Two made little or no reference to it at all. Among the others one spoke of reviewing arrangements for academic staff, and of arrangements for clerical and technical staff. Its more positive stress was on generous study leave conditions and the £70,000 a year replacement teaching budget – 'a very effective investment in the development of staff'. Another introduced staff development in the context of appraisal, referring to departmental, central and external provision. A third identified one and a half full-time staff engaged in the organization and stimulation of staff development and training. It too referred to study leave arrangements, and looked to staff development with appraisal to improve performance and commitment as well as to assist the management of change.

Of the remaining two universities in this group, one referred to appraisal, job satisfaction and working to the main strengths of academic staff, and to increased investment in staff development over the past two years, with further, but unspecified, investment to follow:

> As another means of staff development ... we propose to expand the use of joint appointments with other institutions and of flexible forms of contract allowing staff to spend time in non-university-funded activities.

The other recorded an increase of its academic staff development and training (ASDT) budget to £11,000 in 1988–9, the setting up of a new committee and the appointment of a part-time staff development coordinator. A policy was devised and efforts were made to increase awareness of the importance of ASDT. One is struck, again, by the recency of the effort, and by the large relative increase but still very modest absolute investment in SDT.

Another modern university is more forceful:

> the University is committed to staff development and has acknowledged the crucial role it will play in assisting the delivery of the academic plan by the appointment of a full-time Academic Staff Development Officer and the establishment of sub-committees of the Staffing Committee to deal with academic and non-academic staff development ....
>
> Some £120,000 per year is allocated to the Academic Staff Development Unit to cover central staffing and operating costs; these are expected to increase as activities grow. However, the personal development of staff is a central responsibility of all Deans, Directors and Heads of Department both academic and non-academic, and much staff development will take place within faculties and departments .... Both faculties and non-academic departments will budget for staff development and the University will ensure that the resources necessary to deliver it will rise during the planning period.

All the former colleges of advanced technology profess serious commitment to staff development, although only two specify the resources committed. A third claims 'a substantial investment' since 1986. A staff development unit and key appointments contribute to 'the development of a comprehensive and distinctive staff development programme'. Of the former two, one will at least maintain the current level of staff resource of one full-time Staff Development Adviser (currently half-funded by the EHE Initiative) and the equivalent of approx. half of a Personnel post. It is intended to harness and develop the training skills of other staff.

The training plan and budget under preparation envisaged a possible annual expenditure of £80,000 in 1990–1, and rising. The other claimed an STD programme unsurpassed in the UK university system, with annual expenditure running at £250,000 and higher expenditure visualized, 'recognising that its existing staff are the foundation of its future success'.

Among other former colleges of advanced technology one plans the 'inauguration of staff development schemes which will address the need for both skills training and more fundamental personal development within work settings'. Another locates responsibility within the management development unit, the Director of which draws on the university's CE expertise. In another the activity is managed through the specialist CE department, where there is an academic staff development coordinator. The remit includes providing management training to senior academic staff. Another in this group also makes explicit links with CE expertise. It seeks to provide staff development to equip staff to cope with the expansion of CE, and will also recognize CE in promotion and appraisal criteria. Claiming to be early among universities in developing a comprehensive appraisal and training scheme, it sets out a range of provision including customer care courses for staff dealing with 'customers'. These include students, conference visitors and the general public.

Civic and redbrick commitment to staff development is uniformly clear, although only five are specific about resources, and two refer more generally to them. One mentions 'substantial contributions from central University funds and from individual Faculty budgets'. At another 'the budget for staff development and training is 1 per cent of total salary and wage costs. It is intended that at least 1.5 per cent of salary and wage costs be set aside for staff training by the end of the planning period.' A full-time SDTO was shortly to be appointed. A third tells of a major review in 1989–90 leading to a coordinated approach:

> The establishment of the Staff Development Unit, a key element in both the new staff development programme and in teaching quality assurance, will be increased from three to five professional staff. . . . Over the planning period, expenditure directly attributable to staff development and training is planned to increase by some 25 per cent in real terms (from £310,000 to £390,000 at 1989/90 prices).

Another university will increase the sum spent on staff development to an average of at least 1 per cent of the salary budget, with 'expenditure on key personnel up to £2000 per head per annum' (this statement leaves much room for interpretation). Another university mentions central provision for all aspects of staff training as exceeding £60,000 a year. Here staff development committee policy is administered by a full-time training officer. The only other university to name its staff development price appointed a full-time SDO at the beginning of 1989. It included in its 1990–1 budget about £110,000 for academic and academic-related staff development and training, apart from many other hard-to-quantify SDT costs such as study leave and departmental expenditure.

At another university a full-scale review was about to occur. This would lead to the appointment of a full-time training officer, with an increasing budget. Another records recent growth in academic staff training, such that an SDO has now been appointed to assist across all categories of staff. 'Our clear intention is to sustain the momentum of this important activity.' Another effected a significant change for the 1987–8 academic year, with an ASDT centre and a new director.

A large civic university set up a staff development unit in October 1989, to run its own provision as well as (like a number of others) explicitly to collaborate with the CVCP's SDTU. At another similar university provision will be 'enhanced and regularised', and the personnel office strengthened accordingly, along with a marked (though unspecified) increase in the training budget. Finally, in the university claiming 'the first training and development unit to be established in the UK' this unit plays the leading role in providing 'training tailored to all staff, to maximise personal development and to benefit the institution'.

From staff to organization development

'To benefit the institution.' This brings us back squarely to the title of this chapter: organizational learning as well as individual staff or career development. Few of the extracts above mention the balance (or tension?) between individual and institutional needs. This is implied indirectly by linking staff development with appraisal, and this in turn with quality, especially quality assurance in teaching. On the side of individual motivation there are difficulties in linking development with appraisal: if it appears remedial or punitive the road ahead for staff development will be rocky indeed.

Training and staff development may still be spelt, too often, 'how to teach'. The Hale Report on university teaching methods in the early 1960s found virtually no formal training and instruction in teaching: 'so far as we know Nottingham is the only university at which centrally organised courses of instruction in university teaching are now being provided' (UGC 1964: Chapter 11). According to Marriott,

the 1960s were marked by a rapidly growing concern for the improvement of university teaching methods, and although the evangelical fervour of those days soon died down, through the following decade many universities did introduce formal machinery for academic staff training. Under present conditions of closer external scrutiny and increasing demands for value for money, staff development has been pushed back onto the agenda. The problem is that both conceptually and practically a great deal of ground has to be made up. 'Staff development' in organisations has become a practice of broader significance than is suggested by the conventional emphasis in universities on equipping academics to do their present jobs better.... Quite clearly, it must extend well beyond the academic resources of the institution narrowly and traditionally defined. And, equally clearly, to come to full fruition, it must be undertaken within a framework of strategic planning.

Marriott 1988: 93–4

This 'pushing back on to the agenda' has been narrated above. There is no disputing its reappearance. On the other hand, the resources dedicated to staff development are often unspecified; commonly not separately identified and known; and where they are known and stated, generally only a tiny proportion of the total budget. A knowledge-based industry like HE might in the dying years of the twentieth century be expected to spend several percentage points of its payroll on staff, or human resource, development. Where budgets exist, they are mostly fractions of one percentage point.

Marriott identifies problems with the present perception and scope of staff development. A small circle of enthusiasts is still surrounded by larger numbers of the sceptical and indifferent. Shifting these attitudes involves changing perceptions of what the university is, and of what academic staff membership may imply and require of its full-time academic members. Is it a guild or an organization?

Marriott (1988), a member of the research group, drew on a DES-funded study of staff development for continuing education in universities published in the following year (Bilham *et al.* 1989) and based on experience in six universities and a university college:

Members undertook extensive enquiries into the present state and aspirations of their own universities, and not only in relation to continuing education; the result was an awareness of the common problems confronting universities in an age of stressful change, but also a heightened sense of the particularity of, and the vast complex multidimensional differences between, universities.

Marriott 1988: 90

The focus of enquiry thus became how staff development might assist strategic development: 'external circumstances are coming to require of staff a mission well beyond what the academic tradition has equipped them for' (Marriott 1988: 91–2). The staff development study thus went well beyond CE:

The central theme of this report is the use of staff development, broadly conceived, to initiate and sustain change. Many continuing education staff have experience of producing strategic training programmes for client organisations, involving the clarification of future purposes and objectives, identification of training needs within this framework and encouragement to staff at all levels to see the training function as a key support of organisational change . . . . Such experience needs to be turned back into the parent institutions themselves.

'The way ahead' included:

> a review of current thinking and experience in staff development, with tactful reference to lessons that might be learned from outside the university sector . . ., an analysis of what will be expected of all staff if the mission [of the university] is to be effectively discharged . . . . Thus a strategy is much more than a statement of good intentions, or a declaration of policy within the institution's system of academic governance. It involves a practical commitment to carrying the business through.
>
> Bilham *et al.* 1989: 4–5

The context and need were set by the sharp challenge which the circumstances of the 1980s presented to universities' sense of continuity:

> Reductions in real levels of public financial support and pressure to diversify sources of income have reinforced the sense of a loss of public and political confidence. This is combined with new forms of appraisal, performance measurement and accountability. Many university staff regard the future without enthusiasm despite the positive opportunities the situation can offer for innovation.
>
> Bilham *et al.* 1989: 6

So the study, initially only of staff development for CE, was forced to confront questions about the nature and management of universities: strategic and business plans; mission or, as has more recently appeared among the new discourse, 'vision' statements; and implementation through appropriate leadership, cultures and structures in each distinct institution.

> A statement of purpose by an institution, or mission statement, which is not understood, shared and owned by the institution's members will remain unused. Ideally all staff should clearly understand the mission and feel committed to it. This includes considering the institution first, and its will and capability to turn intentions into actions. It also recognises the links between the total institution and the staff who make it work . . . . Staff development makes sense and is effective only in a context of organisation development . . . . This requires a sense of purpose and direction which is known, shared and owned by all members of the institution.
>
> Bilham *et al.* 1989: 8

The report implied how difficult and controversial this may be:

> All organisations depend on the quality and motivation of the people who work in them, but this is crucially true of universities . . . . In the discussions of the classical nature of a university, the organisation as such is only a background presence, and the progress of universities is

presented as something to be achieved through the ideals of unfettered authority and critical enquiry, within a structure of intellectual authority and collegiality . . . .

Traditionally most academic staff have little concerned themselves with the university as the organisational form which made their professional activities possible. It was simply the backdrop . . . . The university is the theatre in which all our dramas take place, and it is increasingly important that all staff, and not just those who are eager to participate in management, should be conscious of the corporate viability of the places in which they work . . . .

It could be said that too much is being claimed here for 'staff development'. Plainly we are concerned with 'organisational development' and the move towards strategic thinking on a more corporate basis. Yet the desired shift in an organisation will depend on a major effort of staff training in a broad sense.

Bilham et al. 1989: 12, 14

Individuals and organizations

This report moves our attention decisively from the satisfaction of individual learning needs in isolation to the enhancement of institutional capacity to manage and thrive in a new environment. The dichotomy may appear artificial: the learning and change that are required must take place within individuals but as a result the organization develops. In its capacity to engage with and adapt, indeed to proact, to new circumstances, organizational learning occurs. The difficulty is not so much with the concept of organizational learning as with the individualism of university scholars, and the threat that notions of organizational mission and strategic planning present to that individualism:

> We are already in a political and financial climate where it is important for all staff to have a care for how their institutions stand, and for as many as possible to be directly involved in maintaining and improving that position. The CVCP code of practice emphasises individual responsibility within the institutional framework; that is proper and at the same time over-cautious.

Marriott 1988: 95

University staff can no longer take the university for granted, treating it merely as the backdrop. Survival in an inhospitable environment demands a measure of understanding, identification and effort that was previously unnecessary and is still no doubt unpalatable, if not inconceivable, to many academic staff. The positions of the different universities in writing about staff development are cautious and generally ambivalent. Few are explicit about what may follow as staff development in the post-Jarratt UFC era becomes more firmly established. Some universities may avoid altering their expectations of their staff, but these may soon be few.

University staff may in turn come to make demands on their employers for career development and for the acquisition of new knowledge and skills to play new roles, as for example in CE. Training is still mostly a minimalist activity:

> In a community such as a university, and in a community that wishes to remain identifiably a university, staff development broadly and flexibly conceived has to be one of the key responses to the imperatives of surviving, adapting and evolving.
>
> Marriott 1988: 101

It may not be necessary to write and sing a company song. Yet the notion of 'good citizen' (mentioned in perhaps only one planning statement to the UFC), as well as good teacher, is likely to begin jostling the notion of good researcher and good scholar more vigorously, possibly finding its way into the practices as well as the criteria of academic promotion. Development and training need to prepare staff for this as well as for better teaching and research. Staff development will grow and be judged in the context of organizational learning and development.

The connection is by no means obvious or uncontested. An international study of lifelong learning and higher education in 1985 made no mention of organization or staff development, or of institutional learning; it touched only briefly on the crucial subject of changing institutions (Knapper and Cropley 1985). Collegiality and individualism may be thought sacrosanct. Yet the Jarratt Report and the managerialism of polytechnics alongside the universities will not just go away. Conceived and developed with sensitivity to the culture and traditions of universities, staff development could assist them better to manage their environment and advance their special purposes, without turning to anti-collegial and hierarchical modes.

We have been considering how, and how far, universities may be changing. The Enterprise in Higher Education (EHE) initiative of the Training Agency (now TEED) provides another example of intervention, albeit through the persuasion and temptation of million-pound development funds for 'enterprise' rather than by dictat. A number of universities refer to EHE in their bids to the UFC, mainly in the context of curriculum innovation but also with regard to staff development, for EHE is an exercise in organization, often via staff, development. Other government-driven influences and interventions include academic staff appraisal and quality assurance, especially in university teaching. It is too soon to guess how effective a lever for change staff development will prove to be. It may limp along as a feeble and marginal activity. It has been thus hitherto, not something for the fit and well. Conversely it could become a tool of 'neo-macho' management, riding in on the back of staff appraisal as an alternative to or a respite prior to termination of contract. Neither outcome would help universities very much to adapt to the new circumstances and opportunities (for a revised mission as lifelong learning centres) that the next century may bring.

A happier scenario will present itself if staff and career development come to be seen in their multifarious forms (training courses being but one minor element) as the means whereby the whole institution continuously learns and adapts towards purposes agreed and valued by its members. Traditional collegiality and modern organization development might then come into union. Even 'the college' is changing, however. That is to say, the boundaries and membership of 'the university' are no longer what we tend to assume them to be. I will consider these matters further in the final chapter, and draw together the different threads of this study.

8 | The Fallacy of the Ivory Tower

The place of metaphor

Metaphors are a temptation. Scott's throwaway 'menopausal university' (Scott 1984: 8) has not caught on; and I will avoid the 'Janus university' that this book might suggest. The 'ivory tower' has, however, captured popular imagination and survived into the 1990s. This chapter shows how misleading a term it is – not because it is groundless, for without some grounding in fact it would not have flourished as it has. However, its very existence as a metaphor has made it a factor, an influence, in the experience and evolution of universities.

In Britain the ivory tower is part of the confused and complex 'portrait' of universities (and now more broadly of higher education) that has entered the public domain through the writing, and televised dramas, of authors like Tom Wilt, David Lodge and Andrew Davies. 'Within the club', Laurie Taylor's *THES* column has amused (lightly self-mocking) academics while offending the more anxious who fear that 'real damage could be done with those who read the *THES* in Whitehall'. As a metaphor and epithet the ivory tower misleads because the reality is more confused, and more complicated than the term implies. Previous chapters have made this quite clear.

Knapper and Cropley remind us 'how many contemporary educational institutions and systems have been influenced by traditions that emanated from the great medieval European universities'. Despite the 'distinctive patterns of higher education in different nations ... note the considerable similarities in the philosophy, organisation and approaches to teaching in universities throughout the world'. The similarities and convergences have been reinforced by European and United States domination over much of the world: 'this means that many of the central issues in modern education transcend national or regional boundaries' (Knapper and Cropley 1985: 13). In examining the British university scene of the early 1990s we are addressing largely universal phenomena, although particular manifestations, the pace and other details of change, vary from system to system and also, if less, between HEIs within the one system.

The North–South imperialism implied above is reflected, with different distortions of the mirror, in other imperialisms within the education system, and also within HE. It is often felt that the vocational oppresses the liberal, and the economic the cultural; that short-term viability obscures the larger vision. In a society conscious of status and history the old tends to impose itself on the new – old institutions but also old assumptions and practices. The formal education system marginalizes and takes value from the non-formal; credentialling devalues non-award-bearing programmes. We need to recognize these forces in taking stock of competing values, old metaphors, and new paradigms.

The perils of privilege

At one level there is little dispute. All could agree that universities are 'in the service' of the societies which nurture them. Those who inhabit the universities would claim a valid and important role. The relatively modern service or service station metaphor born in North America can claim an ancient lineage. Universities always have some kind of relationship with their societies, and have met a need that functional analysis will quickly reveal. If 'service' in this sense is timeless, so perhaps is a dialectic: between integration with and separation from society. A.H. Halsey, a great Oxford don whose life work has been dedicated to the condition of the world in which he lives, still argued in an annual Radcliffe Lecture at the University of Warwick that dons should not expect to be fully of, or well rewarded by, the modern materialistic world: their privilege and calling implied a measure of austerity. The monastic tradition is recognizable, however faintly, in the Oxbridge collegiate tradition even if celibacy is celebrated, at least in fiction, through its absence.

In the Dark Ages monasteries preserved the culture and achievements of the past through difficult times for unborn generations. Few would deny the service of monastic scribes to society and civilization. For some, contemporary society is a new dark age. From this perspective withdrawal may appear the best way for universities to serve society in the long term: cultural preservation and transmission through grim times. Some argue that universities should draw back, contracting their size and increasing their poverty, so as to remain true to their mission.

The question can be located less dramatically within Coombs's perception of a 'world crisis in education' brought on by the huge increase in numbers in and demand for education since the mid-twentieth century (Coombs 1968, 1985). The massification of education, primary (still an aspiration in many poor countries), then secondary, and ultimately, as already in the advanced industrialized systems, tertiary or higher, means changing the existing educational institutions. Is it replacement or re-creation, replication or transformation? The increasing demand for higher education raises questions about the role of universities and their contribution to society. It is not clear that the present system in the UK where leading universities select one in every fifteen or twenty-five applicants makes best sense politically or socially. Instability threatens such an arrangement – especially in a property-owning democracy which goes to the polls every few years.

An inherently volatile situation has been made more unstable by some of the more active academic staff, and also by late sixties student activism. Scholars and intellectuals claim a unique duty and a privilege (academic freedom) to be critics of contemporary society and its values. For a brief spell some students and staff combined to try to change both the university and the world. The 'world crisis in education' was sharpened for HE in the seventies by dislike of and loss of confidence in what universities got up to with the young. The reaction triggered two decades of sociologist-bashing.

An economic pendulum also swung back to deal HE a blow. Economic difficulties became entangled with doubts about the public return on invest-ment, particularly in higher education. The arguments and the psychological swings about the economic benefits of HE and about who gains and who should pay are important for the trials and fortunes of HE. Note how precarious the position of the university becomes: (a) when it appears to monopolize a scarce good (high quality degrees as meal tickets); (b) when this monopoly looks costly to an aggressively cost-containing administration of strong free market persuasion; (c) when the university presumes (from a basis of academic tenure resented by the more vulnerable and the unem-ployed, and pilloried by a radical-populist press) to teach from its pedestal the rights and shortcomings of society and the state.

Withdrawal into the world of letters – monastic detachment and ascetic poverty – is one thing. It may provide little threat and be tolerated, even admired. To claim to be above and beyond society, while living well at the public expense from an unassailable monopoly, and yet heavily engaged with it as self-appointed critic and judge – this is another and altogether more dangerous thing. The modern university has tried to have the best of every-thing. Its control over credentialling, in a meritocratic, competitive, nominal-ly open society, and so its stake in social reproduction, jars with the pulpit posture.

A safer anchorage?

When one reflects thus on what the modern university does and what some of its members seek for it to be, it becomes more clear how plural, perhaps dangerously and untenably plural, its functions and purposes are. Detach-ment – the ivory tower – then looks less like arrogance, more like that discretion which is the better part of valour. However, the pendulum has swung inexorably back from separation to engagement with society. The only way forward through the 'crisis of the university' is by way of more clearly anchored, explained and agreed involvement.

The learning centre paradigm offers a viable alternative to the ivory tower. It provides a legitimate basis for the continuing health, expansion and diversification of the university system (not therefore necessarily for each individual university). It holds out promise of common ground on which the public policy prescriptions of efficiency, economy, access, quality and accountability can live in reasonable harmony with the values and purposes which, for all the perturbations and exceptions, have characterized 'the academy' throughout the generations, and which continue to provide a common culture and shared discourse for international gatherings of scholars and administrators from university systems the world over.

Lifelong learning for recurrent education – the notion of being a resource centre for the learning society – could thus clarify the role and nature of the modern university. It could give it a legitimacy which is comprehended and acceptable both to its membership and to its masters: politicians, public, the Treasury.

> In fact many colleges and universities already claim to promote life-
> long learning through existing teaching programmes, and the terms
> 'lifelong learning' and 'lifelong education' have become favourite themes
> in institutional publicity.
>
> Knapper and Cropley 1985: 15

This was true of the United States in the mid-1980s but still not true five years later of Britain. Only one university clearly adopted the term in describing its objectives and plans to the UFC in 1990, although it and the ideas behind it have become commoner in calls to the education system among which employers' voices are increasingly clear. Knapper and Cropley (1985: 15) remark that the expression has been taken over by many HEIs 'to describe familiar activities and programmes that have existed for many years (such as part-time study or off-campus courses) and owes little to recent theoretical discussions of lifelong learning'. Surely this matters not. Indeed these authors a little later find that 'one way of looking at lifelong education is to regard it as a rationalisation of a number of existing trends in contemporary theory and practice' (Knapper and Cropley 1985: 16).

A new paradigm is a way of seeing differently what is already familiar. It grows up unrecognized as a host in the frame of the old before emerging well-formed into view. The transition to the new potentially managerialist HE world of the 1990s is tough enough as it is for many in the greying community of scholars. Resentment at the need for change is widespread, sometimes bitter, as correspondence to the *THES* regularly reveals. The value of the new paradigm will lie in its power to rationalize, legitimate, and give form and purpose to what may seem to be the random and wilful imposition of successive ill-explained innovations. If much in the new paradigm is familiar, so much the better.

A choice of futures

This book is about 'the other continuing education': those forms which are included in the broadest use of the term (in Unesco and OECD adult education) but excluded from CE as defined by the Universities Funding Council for purposes of financial and administrative convenience (though included in the wider definition of the UGC/CE Working Party in 1984). The principle of recurrent education for lifelong learning goes beyond both narrow and broader definitions of CE. It runs back into the school system and into teacher education, spilling over also beyond schools and the formal education system into society's other institutions and arrangements.

Checklists of changes required to bring together the elements of a lifelong learning system have been compiled over quite some years, and not just in Britain. Duke's 1976 study concluded with a list of forty-three suggested developments for Australia. The contents pages of Knapper and Cropley's international study published in 1985 (notably Chapters 4 to 6) themselves read like such an inventory. They list in turn teaching and learning activities; the role of instructors; evaluation and certification; new approaches including distance learning, linking education and work, individualized, independent and peer learning; and strategies for changing teaching and learning methods as well as institutional policy. They attempt to bring together ideas and practices which 'although possessing an inherent unity' would, without an ordering principle or paradigm, continue to be treated separately (Knapper and Cropley 1985: 17–18).

The UGC's 1984 report on continuing education was left on the shelf. Many universities were still struggling after the 1981 cuts. The UGC, despite the existence of a toothless joint NAB/UGC Standing Committee on Continuing Education, seemed to have no stomach for continuing education. These were difficult years for what has historically been identified as the heartland of university continuing education. Core budgets of the extramural departments (EMDs) for liberal adult education from the DES were squeezed. The old departments sought both to adapt and, sometimes, to stay the same, much like their parent institutions. Most tended to acquire new functions by accretion: enlarged responsibilities for professional updating or PICKUP, then perhaps for access work and for part-time degrees, sometimes explorations and developments in areas like modularization and CAT, APEL and staff development.

The EMDs are outside the main frame of this book. They provide an exquisite microcosm of the problems of identity and adaptation which the 1980s thrust upon British universities as a whole; and of the need for a fresh rationale or paradigm with which to explain and order apparently diffuse, maybe very diverse, roles and tasks.

What universities told the Funding Council was much more clear and confident than the preceding paragraphs, and much writing on the 'crisis' in, or of, education or the university worldwide would lead one to expect. Discounting for the circumstances (the UFC would be unlikely to value academic equivocation on strategic and business plans) one is still left with a sense that universities at the level of top management have come to terms with the new world and can see ways to 'thrive on chaos' (Peters 1987).

Large uncertainties remain. How hard will government push universities down the road of expanding student numbers with only marginally more public income, presumably on a fees-only basis? How will the separate funding of research work out in the future? Will more university research migrate into separate research institutes? Will that sacred cow, the inseparability of university teaching from research, finally be slain? Will older students and their employers find in the future that universities genuinely work in partnership to meet their needs, continuously adapting admissions criteria, curricula, teaching and delivery methods and course assessment?

University heads had drawn closer to their polytechnic counterparts and a *modus vivendi* was being worked out at this level even before the 1991 HE White Paper spelt the end of the binary divide. The transition to 'diversity within unity' will make an interesting comparison with the decisive top-down demolition of binarism in Australia.

Peter Scott suggested of the polytechnics a few years ago that

> perhaps in the end the only adequate 'polytechnic' philosophy for higher education is no philosophy at all, to come to terms with the inevitable and perhaps enriching heterodoxy of intellectual activity once it has escaped from the gravity of the university.
>
> Scott 1984: 14

Does this now mean a British polytechnic 'takeover' of the universities within a new and enriching heterodoxy?

Dismantling the tower

Much of all this concerns policy and is for institutional leadership. It can also be largely on the surface. Becher's 'academic tribes' (Becher 1989) still thrive beyond the boardroom, protected by the resistant band of middle management which obstructs change in formal organizations. In-house and regional staff development programmes commonly feature courses for heads of departments. Tribalism and academic individualism will give the innovators a good run for their money, as one senior lecturer promises in a letter to the *THES* (15 February 1991):

> There are tens of thousands of us out here who are determined that appraisal will be marginalised to become a 'meaningless annual chore'..... The structural changes themselves cannot be resisted, but the results they were designed to achieve can be effectively thwarted. That is what we have achieved for line-management and appraisal, and academic audit will be similarly deflected ....
>
> It is comforting to those of us here in the University of Glasgow to know that the academic ethos which has sustained us for the last 540 years has not been totally subverted, even in the Staff Development and Training Unit of the CVCP.

The letter concludes with a reference to 'the present invasion of our profession by alien amateurs', which 'merely costs our time and the salaries of a few supernumerary staff development officers'.

In a world of turbulence and diversity concepts and assumptions can be pitifully static. We can think of higher education in this way. Some institutions are ancient, federal or collegiate. Others have grown through modern mergers. They may have several campuses. Others again have downtown or outreach centres, usually initially under CE or extramural management. University farms, experimental stations and other field sites belong in a different compartment of the mind. The geographical dispersal of some polytechnics, with many buildings miles apart, might signal a message. We talk about levelling the playing field, about government moving the goalposts. The idea of identifiable teams, dressed distinctively and set apart from the spectators, remains strong – although Oxford scarves and Harvard sweatshirts are available to all buyers!

To return to the more familiar metaphor of the ivory tower, the walls of the university have been breached, comprehensively and irreparably. Universities are abandoning the name extramural for their CE departments. Much CE no longer takes place outside the walls. Conversely, more of the 'regular' teaching of the university from which CE will become indistinguishable as modularization gathers pace and part- and full-time students sit down together will take place 'outside the walls'. CE departments are 'transmural'. They build bridges and face both out and in. It might be more accurate still to think of them as pulling down the walls, helping the invaders by steadying the siege ladders. Some CE staff claim to do 'inreach' – taking new ideas and clienteles into the institution, not just selling courses at an off-licence round the back. To stay with this metaphor, abolishing licensing hours makes it possible to study when and wherever one wants and can afford to – not just when, where and as licensed by authority.

Opening up club membership

Transforming the EMDs, making all academic departments transmural rather than polarizing the internal from the extramural, is one obvious example of bringing down the walls. What about the membership of the university? Those on the payroll may together greatly outnumber the (full-time, tenured) academic staff. Many planning statements specify different groups and categories of staff. A few directly acknowledge the crucial public relations and 'gatekeeper' roles played by some humble low-status employees. Student activism twenty years ago brought home to institutional managements that students too were members of the academic community. They were then widely included in institutions' decision-making structures, albeit and perhaps unintendedly with the result of co-opting student leadership and absorbing its energies.

This is barely the tip of the iceberg. The membership of the academic community is moving further and further from the celibate residential college community in which the gold standard degree is still sub-consciously anchored. Students are counted in FTEs (full-time equivalents). The number of individuals enrolled as students far exceeds that of those instinctively referred to by administrations still thinking in terms of full-time degree programmes.

The UFC's Aims included continuing, part-time and mature age students. The requirements it places on universities will doubtless help to change the culture and assumptions. Associate student schemes, the onward march of modularization and with it increased single unit study will add to the numbers who can claim membership of one or another academic community. Then there are those who associate with a university through its science park, scholarly societies, arts centre or sporting facilities – and may choose to see themselves in one sense or another as 'enrolled' as learners at the institution. Treading belatedly in the steps of the OU, increasing numbers of institutions offer MBA and other courses in an external mode. Others bring people on campus for intensive study periods leading to the award of a higher degree, such as a modular Master of Science via an Integrated Graduate Development Scheme (IGDS) in partnership with industry.

Nor is this all. I noted in Chapter 6 the various forms of institutional association, many of them changing rapidly, in the FHE system. Ingenious new forms will be devised, short of the full mergers, amalgamations or takeovers that are part of past growth and present aspirations. Partnership between HE and industry takes many forms, including teaching companies, consortium arrangements, property development and individual, course and institutional sponsorship. Consortia were highly favoured in Britain in the late 1980s. They have become somewhat less visible and may prove mainly a temporary mode of development, although some remain active (see Sofo 1990 for an Australian view of British consortia)

Increasingly important for enhancing access and breaking down the boundaries of some institutions is the cluster of arrangements known as validation, affiliation and franchising. Further and higher education colleges may associate or affiliate with universities and polytechnics – the former preferred for their higher status, the latter for their greater flexibility. Courses may be validated with or without any wider form of association. Students whose courses are validated gain degrees and diplomas of the validating institution, be it the CNAA or the University of Leeds or Manchester. The membership of these academic communities is thus both widened and blurred. Where courses are franchised to a local college the first year of a degree of a polytechnic or university may be taught in more accessible and 'user-friendly' FE; students move on in later years to the senior partner institution. By such an arrangement the HEI effectively acquires (with minimal responsibility) a number of outreach centres or subsidiary campuses, and an enlarged student roll.

Franchising is often associated with a prior access-type year, especially into science and technology. The result resembles two plus two arrangements where four-year open access honours degree programmes are designed jointly between HE and FE, the students spending half their time in each place. Again, students 'belong' to the HEI from the first day – and in principle the HEI belongs to them as it does to the young full-time undergraduate 'living in'.

More and more HEIs are getting to grips with APEL. Some are already validating educational programmes run by employers, which give advanced standing via credit transfer into their degrees. As these become regular partnerships rather than merely one-off *ad hoc* cases it becomes increasingly hard to say where the line should be drawn between those who are and those who are not students of the HEI. No department tutor or registry officer would doubt that 'year-abroad' full-time students away in Europe or the USA are still one's own students; likewise sandwich course students on industrial placement.

This is visualized in the following passage:

> the relationship between different learning settings such as factories, programmes offered by professional associations, colleges, and universities would alter in such a way that boundaries between them would become 'porous' – learners would transfer back and forth between settings, or select various mixtures of settings .... Many settings not normally regarded as having a substantial educational role, such as museums or zoos, libraries, radio stations, churches, committee rooms and so on, would have their contribution to purposeful learning acknowledged and emphasised.
>
> Knapper and Cropley 1985: 34

This was presented hypothetically. It may have seemed far-fetched as recently as the mid-eighties. It might still cause apoplexy in some senior common rooms. It does not, however, look so far-fetched in the light of the APEL, CAT, modularization and competency debates, and movements. As more and more people one way or another gain access to the university and become, in one way or another, part of its 'student body', HEIs do become centres for lifelong learning, and their membership becomes less and less determinate.

Thus boundaries and membership rules get fuzzy among students. The same is true, and perhaps more significant still, of academic staff. The guild or college gets less and less exclusive. Some planning statements allude to mobilizing and strengthening non-traditional part-time staff. Almost all universities (and polytechnics ahead of them) are loosening their meaning of 'faculty'. Professional and industrial personnel enjoy faculty status. They teach part-time in professional and technological areas. Workplace supervision of trainee teachers and of sandwich engineers in training means university workplace teachers by one designation or another; likewise with trainee nurses and doctors in hospitals. It is not unusual to have professional and industrial personnel seconded into a teaching post for a limited term.

More widely, and more from necessity than choice, departments' part-time staff lists grow. Increasing proportions of teaching are done by casual hourly staff or through fractional appointments. Early retired and other older colleagues assist many departments on a salaried or largely honorary basis, taking a more or less active part in the general life of the department as well as doing some of its teaching.

There may be a further implication for continuing full-time academic staff in the post-tenure era – an implication alluded to in earlier chapters by reference to 'non-organizations' and a company song. The identity, health, continuity, sense of purpose and being of a university as well as the resources it wins from the environment will increasingly depend on the understanding, shared purpose, commitment and active energies of the full collegiate core membership; not merely on the men (usually) at the top. There may be lurking in the wings more of a revolution in the role of and requirements on full-time academic staff than selection and promotions committees have yet begun to realize.

More loosely, many members of the (usually local, sometimes national or international) 'community' may be a part of the 'academic community'. They serve on councils and other governing and advisory bodies of different parts of the institution, sometimes contributing actively to making its culture and defining its mission. Some have an influence merely by being there – near-silent reminders by their presence of other worlds and other interests, which modify the behaviour and the decisions of full academic members. One way and another the membership of the academic community has been opened up, its membrane permeated and its culture influenced, in ways that a cursory glance at the annual calendar and UCCA enrolments could scarcely reveal.

Accepting the change

It is not just the calendar and the pass-list but the deeper mindset that must be overcome. One difficulty about accepting change is that change already assimilated and familiar may pass unrecognized. Practical and ethical considerations arise, and possibly compete, when we ask how to facilitate changes of the kind which this book is about. It is not an easy task.

> To repeat the dismal theme of early chapters: much teaching in higher education is of the traditional didactic sort, much learning is passive in nature . . . . The organised support of lifelong learning by means of a system of lifelong education is fraught with difficulties . . . the idea of deliberately setting out to bureaucratise an innovation is itself 'inherently obnoxious'.
>
> Knapper and Cropley 1985: 121, 85

Knapper and Cropley acknowledge that existing institutions will be changed gradually rather than scrapped at the behest of a new idea like lifelong learning. Rather unconvincingly they suggest that adopting a lifelong learning paradigm would mean transforming existing institutions: 'the nature of these transformations would be derived, naturally, from the principles of lifelong education that have already been outlined' (Knapper and Cropley 1985: 63). Later they state, more pragmatically, that

> while lifelong learning is unlikely to produce immediate and radical change in conventional systems of higher education, it makes sense to be on the alert for examples of partial shifts in philosophy and practice that go some way towards fulfilling our goals for this new approach.
>
> Knapper and Cropley 1985: 86

Change in universities is commonly effected more easily by stealth, by sleight of hand, than by mounting the pulpit. A reassuring word understates possible implications. The initial scope of innovation is restricted, with an early review to check on losses as well as gains. There is allusion to similar, harmless and fruitful arrangements at other well known and well regarded institutions. Unethical or cowardly it may be, but instinctively this seems the most practical short-term way of facilitating change with the maximum consensus. At least it is more palatable and more constructive than change brutally imposed from without. Imposed change engenders covert resistance and quiet sabotage – and by whom more subtly and effectively than by highly intelligent, highly principled, highly articulate academics!

Waving the flag of *education permanente*, recurrent education or lifelong learning at every opportunity may not be the best way forward. The ivory tower exists no more, although elements can be traced, half-hidden like illegal tusks in a Hong Kong dealer's yard. As a paradigm rather than a banner, however, easing the university towards becoming a centre for facilitating lifelong learning may have a fairer wind.

Drawing out a paradigm rather than waving a banner means persuading rather than rallying, bullying or hectoring. It should encourage the kind of conversation, the discursive or dialectical process enjoyed in universities, whereby changes already effected can be understood and valued; and changes in train or in the wind can be seen and felt to have coherence and a rationale which, separately, each may lack. We are certainly moving, possibly by now downhill and with accelerating speed, towards adopting a new paradigm for higher education. This is suitably captured in the words lifelong learning, and the meanings resident behind them. 'The revolution is inevitable – so help make the revolution.' Thus might a new paradigm for the modern university emerge – for in a sense, too, it is already here, and waiting for us to see it.

Appendix
UFC-funded Institutions

England	Old	Civic	Redbrick	Greenfield	Ex-CAT	Other
Aston					*	
Bath					*	
Birmingham		*				
Bradford					*	
Bristol		*				
Brunel					*	
Cambridge	*					
City					*	
Durham	*					
East Anglia				*		
Essex				*		
Exeter			*			
Hull			*			
Keele			*			
Kent				*		
Lancaster				*		
Leeds		*				
Leicester			*			
Liverpool		*				
London Business School						*
London						*
Birkbeck						
Goldsmiths'						
Imperial						
Institute of Advanced Legal Studies						
Institute of Education						
King's						
LSE						
School of Pharmacy						

England	Old	Civic	Redbrick	Greenfield	Ex-CAT	Other
Queen Mary's College						
RHBNC						
RVC						
SOAS						
UCL						
Wye						
Federal CE Centre						
Loughborough					*	
Manchester Business School						*
Manchester		*				
UMIST						*
Newcastle			*			
Nottingham		*				
Oxford	*					
Reading			*			
Salford					*	
Sheffield		*				
Southampton			*			
Surrey					*	
Sussex				*		
Warwick				*		
York				*		

Wales
Aberystwyth
Bangor
Cardiff
St David's Lampeter
Swansea
UWCM

Scotland
Aberdeen
Dundee
Edinburgh
Glasgow
Heriot-Watt
St Andrews
Stirling
Strathclyde

Northern Ireland
Queen's Belfast
Ulster

Bibliography

Abrahamsson, K. (1986). *Adult Participation in Swedish Higher Education*. Stockholm, Almqvist & Wiksell International.

ACACE (1982). *Continuing Education: from Policies to Practice*. Leicester, NIACE.

Allen, M. (1988). *The Goals of Universities*. Milton Keynes, Open University Press.

Argyris, C. and Schon, D.A. (1978). *Organizational Learning*. Reading, MA, Addison-Wesley.

Ball, C. (1989). *Aim Higher: Widening Access to Higher Education*. London, RSA.

Ball, C. (1990). *More Means Different. Widening Access in Higher Education*. London, RSA.

Barnett, R. (1990). *The Idea of Higher Education*. Milton Keynes, Open University Press.

Barnett, R. (1991). 'Break-up of a happy marriage', *Times Higher Education Supplement*, 15 March.

Becher, T. (1989). *Academic Tribes and Territories: Intellectual Enquiry and the Cultures of Disciplines*. Milton Keynes, Open University Press.

Berdahl, R., Moodie, G. and Spitzberg, I. (1991). *Quality and Access in Higher Education. Comparing Britain and the United States*. Milton Keynes, Open University Press.

Bilham, T. *et al.* (1989). *Staff Development in Continuing Education*. London, DES.

Birch, W. (1988). *The Challenge to Higher Education: Reconciling Responsibilities to Scholarship and Society*. Milton Keynes, Open University Press.

Bird, R. and Callaghan, A. (1990). *Report of the Review of the Council for Academic Awards*. London, DES.

Boud, D. and Griffin, V. (eds) (1987). *Appreciating Adults Learning: From the Learners' Perspective*. London, Kogan Page.

Bourner, T. and Hamed, M. (1987a). *Entry Qualifications and Degree Performance*. London, CNAA.

Bourner, T. and Hamed, M. (1987b). 'Degree awards in the public sector of higher education: comparative results for A-level entrants and non-A-level entrants', *Journal of Access Studies*, 2(1), 25–41.

Boyd, W.L. and Smart, D. (eds) (1987). *Educational Policy in Australia and America: Comparative Perspectives*. Lewes, Falmer Press.

Brennan, B. (1988). 'It is not necessarily natural: university adult and continuing education in Australia', *International Journal of University Adult Education*, 27(1), 1–22.

Brundin, C. (Chairman) (1990). *Report of the Committee on Continuing Education Policy.* Oxford, University of Oxford.

Byrd, P. and Schuller, T. (1988). 'Parlaying change in education: part-time degrees at the University of Warwick', *Studies in Continuing Education,* 10(2), 125–36.

Calder, J. (1989). 'A study of the relationship between deliberate change by adults and their use of media-based learning materials', DPhil dissertation, University of Oxford.

Campbell, D. (1984). *The New Majority. Adult Learners in the University.* Edmonton, University of Alberta Press.

Cassels, J. (1990). *Britain's Real Skill Shortage.* London, PSI.

Chaplin, T. and Drake, K. (1987). *American Experience of Accreditation of Employee-Provided Training.* Manchester, CONTACT.

CIHE (1987). *Towards a Partnership. Higher Education – Government – Industry.* London, CIHE.

CIHE (1990a). *Towards a Partnership. The Humanities and the Working World.* London, CIHE.

CIHE (1990b). *Collaborative Courses in Higher Education. Expanding the Partnership with Industry.* London, CIHE.

Clarke, K. *et al.* (1991). *Higher Education. A New Framework.* London, HMSO.

Clendon, R. and Yorke, D. (1986). *Towards Effective Contact.* Manchester, CONTACT.

CNAA (1987). *Credit Accumulation and Transfer Scheme: Background Papers.* London, CNAA.

CNAA (1990). *Performance Indicators and Quality Assurance.* London, CNAA.

CNAA (1991). *CNAA Services in Support of Quality in Higher Education* (CIDC/11/9). London, CNAA.

Coldstream, P. (1991). *Higher Education, Industry and the Journey of Learning.* Hull, Hull University Press.

Commission on Post-Secondary Education (1972). *The Learning Society* (pre-publication copy of report). Toronto, Ministry of Government Services.

Committee on Higher Education (1963). *Higher Education. Report* (the Robbins Report), Cmnd. 2154. London, HMSO.

Coombs, P.H. (1968). *The World Educational Crisis: a Systems Analysis.* Oxford, Oxford University Press.

Coombs, P.H. (1985). *The World Crisis in Education. The View from the Eighties.* Oxford, Oxford University Press.

Coopers and Lybrand (1985). *A Challenge to Complacency. Changing Attitudes to Training.* Sheffield, TA (and NEDO).

Cross, K. (1981). *Adults as Learners: Increasing Participation and Facilitating Learning.* San Francisco, Jossey-Bass.

CVCP (1986). *The Future of the Universities.* London, CVCP.

Dave, R.H. (1973). *Lifelong Education and School Curriculum.* Hamburg, UIE.

Dave, R.H. (1975). *Reflections on Lifelong Education and the School.* Hamburg, UIE.

DES (1978). *Higher Education into the 1990s. A Discussion Document.* London, HMSO.

DES (1985). *The Development of Higher Education into the 1990s.* London, HMSO.

DES (1987). *Changes in Structure and National Planning for Higher Education. Contracts between the Funding Bodies and Higher Education Institutions.* London, DES.

DES (1988). Published letter from Robert Jackson to Sir Henry Chilver, 31 October, on the functions of the UFC. London, DES.

DES (1989). *Universities in the Training Market: an Evaluation of the Universities*

Grants Committee PICKUP Selective Funding Scheme (the Geale Report). London, DES.

DES (1991). *Education and Training for the 21st Century*. London, HMSO.

DTI (1990a). *Total Quality Management. A Practical Approach*. London, DTI.

DTI (1990b). *Leadership and Quality Management. A Guide for Chief Executives*. London, DTI.

Duke, C. (1976). *Australian Perspectives on Lifelong Education*. Melbourne, ACER.

Duke, C. (1982). 'Evolution of the recurrent education concept', *International Journal of Lifelong Education*, 1(4), 323–40.

Duke, C. (1988). *The Future Shape of Continuing Education and Universities: an Inaugural Lecture*. Warwick, DCE University of Warwick.

Duke, C. (1989a). 'Research studies in common in adult education', *Adult Education and Development*, 32, 129–58.

Duke, C. (1989b). 'Creating the accessible institution', in O. Fulton (ed.) *Access and Institutional Change*. Milton Keynes, Open University Press, 163–78.

Duke, C. (1990). 'Popularizing mandarin', *Adults Learning*, 1(5), 149–52.

Duke, C. and Marriott, S. (1973). *Paper Awards in Liberal Adult Education*. London, Michael Joseph.

Duke, C. and Moseley, R. (eds) (1990). *Quality and Control: Widening High Quality University Continuing Education Through the Nineties* (UCACE Occasional Paper No. 4). Warwick, UCACE.

Eggar, T. (1991). 'Access to higher education', conference address at the University of Leeds.

Eggins, H. (ed.) (1989). *Restructuring Higher Education*. Milton Keynes, Open University Press.

Emery, F. (ed.) (1969). *Systems Thinking*. London, Penguin.

Evans, N. (1988). *The Assessment of Prior Experiential Learning*. London, CNAA.

Farnes, N. (1990). 'The place and influence of community education in people's lives', PhD dissertation, Cranfield Institute of Technology.

Faure, E. *et al.* (1972). *Learning to Be: the World of Education Today and Tomorrow* (the Faure Report). Paris, Unesco.

Fazaeli, T. (1991). *Innovation in Access*. Leicester, NIACE for UDACE.

Field, J. (1988). 'Does homogeneity mean quality in higher education? A study of younger undergraduate perceptions of mature students', *Journal of Access Studies*, 3(2), 38–47.

Field, J. (1989). 'Mature students in the undergraduate commmunity: what kind of special case?', *Pastoral Care in Education*, 7(3), 16–18.

Fulton, O. (ed.) (1989). *Access and Institutional Change*. Milton Keynes, Open University Press.

Fulton, O. and Ellwood, S. (1989). *Admission to Higher Education. Policy and Practice*. Sheffield, Training Agency.

Gardner, P. and Pickering, J. (1991). 'Learning with yuppies or, on counselling mature students'. *Pastoral Care in Education*, 9(1), 13–19.

Hameyer, U. (1979). *School Curriculum in the Context of Lifelong Learning*. Hamburg, UIE.

HMI (1991). *Education for Adults. A Review by HMI*. London, HMSO.

Holmberg, B. (1989). *Theory and Practice of Distance Education*. London, Routledge.

Hopper, E. and Osborn, M. (1975). *Adult Students: Education, Selection and Social Control*. London, Frances Pinter.

Houghton, V. and Richardson, K. (eds) (1974). *Recurrent Education. A Plea for Lifelong Learning*. London, Ward Lock Educational.

Howarth, A. (1991). 'Learning without walls', paper presented to CATS Conference (Kellogg Forum, Oxford).

Hunter, C. and Keehn, M. (eds) (1985). *Adult Education in China*. London, Croom Helm.

Husen, T. (1974). *The Learning Society*. London, Methuen.

Husen, T. (1986). *The Learning Society Revisited. Essays*. Oxford, Pergamon.

Illich, I. and Verne, J. (1976). *Imprisoned in the Global Classroom*. London, Writers and Readers Publishing Cooperative.

Jackson, R. (1990). 'Thoughts on re-reading Newman's idea of a university', Centenary Conference address, University of St Andrews.

James, D. *et al.* (1989). *Adults in Higher Education: a Policy Discussion Paper*. Leicester, NIACE.

Jarratt, A. (Chairman) (1985). *Report of the Steering Committee for Efficiency Studies in Universities*. London, CVCP.

Johns, D. (1990). *A Vision of the Future*. Warwick, UCACE.

Johnson, R. and Hinton, F. (1986). *It's Human Nature. Non-Award Adult and Continuing Education in Australia*. Canberra, CTEC.

Jones, D.R. and Anwyl, J. (eds) (1987). *Privatizing Higher Education. A New Australian Issue*. Melbourne, University of Melbourne.

Kelly, T. (1991). *Developing Wider Access to Universities*. London, DES.

Kim, L. (1982). *Widening Admission to Higher Education in Sweden – the 25/5 Scheme. A Study of the Implementation Process*. Stockholm, National Board of Universities and Colleges.

Knapper, C. and Cropley, A. (1985). *Lifelong Learning and Higher Education*. London, Croom Helm.

Loder, C. (ed.) (1990). *Quality Assurance and Accountability in Higher Education*. London, Kogan Page.

McPherson, A. (1990). 'Access', paper prepared for Leverhulme Seminar on the Future of High Education: a Reassessment, London, Birkbeck College.

Manpower Services Commission (1987). *Enterprise in Higher Education*. Sheffield, MSC.

Marriott, S. (1981). *A Backstairs to a Degree: Demands for an Open University in late Victorian England*. Leeds, University of Leeds DAE.

Marriott, S. (1984). *Extramural Empires: Service and Self-interest in English University Adult Education, 1873–1983*. Nottingham, University of Nottingham DAE.

Marriott, S. (1988). 'Staff Development for PICKUP', in T. Bilham *et al.* (eds) *The PICKUP Papers*. London, DES.

Moser, C. (1991). 'A vision beyond blinkers', *Guardian*, 8 January.

NAB/UGC (1984). *Higher Education and the Needs of Society*, Joint Statement by the NAB and the UGC. London, NAB and UGC.

Neave, M. (1991). *Models of Quality Assurance in Europe*. London, CNAA.

Newman, J. (1852). *The Idea of a University* (1965 edn). London, Dent.

OECD (1973). *Recurrent Education: a Strategy for Lifelong Learning*. Paris, OECD.

OECD (1981). *Intergovernmental Conference on Policies for Higher Education in the 1980s. Overview of Issues*. Paris, OECD.

OECD (1983). *Policies for Higher Education in the 1980s*. Paris, OECD.

OECD (1986). *The Role and Functions of Universities*. Paris, OECD (published as *Universities Under Scrutiny*, OECD, 1987).

OECD (1989a). *Higher Education and Employment: the Changing Partnership. Recent Developments in Continuing Professional Education*. Paris, OECD.

OECD (1989b). *Higher Education and Employment. Higher Education and the Changing Employment Prospects*. Paris, OECD.

OECD (1989c). *Alternatives to Universities in Higher Education. Country Study. Federal Republic of Germany*. Paris, OECD.

OECD (1990a). *Higher Education in California*. Paris, OECD.

OECD (1990b). *High Quality Education and Training for All*. Paris, OECD.

Otter, S. (1989). *Student Potential in Britain*. Leicester, UDACE.

Palfreyman, D. (1989). 'The Warwick way: a case study of entrepreneurship within a university context', *Entrepreneurship and Regional Development*, 1, 207–19.

Parry, G. (1989). *Access and Preparatory Courses Offered by or in Association with the Universities*. London, SCUE.

Parry, G. (1990). *Engineering Futures*. London, Engineering Council.

Parry, G. and Davies, P. (1991). *Framework Features*. Interim report on the ACRG system. Leicester, UDACE.

PCFC (1990). 'Widening participation in higher education', Circular to directors/ principals. London, PCFC.

Pedley, M., Boydell, T. and Burgoyne, J. (1989). 'Towards the learning company', *Management Education and Development*, 20(1), 1–8.

Perry, P. (1990). 'Celebrating the end of elitism', *Guardian*, 11 September.

Peters, T. (1987). *Thriving on Chaos*. London, Macmillan.

Reid, E. (1990). 'Access: an institutional perspective', paper prepared for Leverhulme Seminar on the Future of Higher Education: Reassessment, London, Birkbeck College.

Robbins, Lord (1966). *The University in the Modern World*. London, Macmillan.

Robinson, E. (1968). *The New Polytechnics*. London, Cornmarket.

Rockhill, K. (1983). *Academic Excellence and Public Service*. New Brunswick, Transaction Books.

Roderick, G., Bell, J. and Hamilton, S. (1982). 'Unqualified mature students in British universities', *Studies in Adult Education*, 14, 59–68.

Roderick, G.W. and Stephens, M.D. (1984). *Post-School Education*. London, Croom Helm.

RSA (1988). *Raising the Standard. Wider Access to Higher Education*. London, RSA/ Industry Matters.

Sargant, N. *et al.* (1990). *Learning Throughout Adult Life*. Leicester, NIACE.

Schlossberg, N. *et al.* (1989). *Improving Higher Education Environments for Adults*. San Francisco, Jossey-Bass.

Schuller, T. (1990a). 'The exploding community? The university idea and the smashing of the academic atom', *Oxford Review of Education*, 16(1), 3–14.

Schuller, T. (1990b). 'Small a access and the structure of higher education', *Adults Learning*, 2(4), 97–8.

Schuller, T. and Megarry, J. (eds) (1979). *Recurrent Education and Lifelong Learning*. New York, NP.

Schuller, T., Tight, M. and Weil, S. (1988). 'Continuing education and the redrawing of boundaries', *Higher Education Quarterly*, 42(4), 335–52.

Schutze, H. (ed.) (1987). *Adults in Higher Education: Policies and Practice in Great Britain and North America*. Stockholm, Almqvist & Wiksell International.

Scott, P. (1984). *The Crisis of the University*. London, Croom Helm.

Shattock, M. (1991). *Making a University. A Celebration of Warwick's First 25 Years*. Coventry, University of Warwick.

Silver, H. and Brennan, J. (1988). *A Liberal Vocationalism*. London, Methuen.

Slowey, M. (1988). 'Adult students: the new mission for higher education?', *Higher Education Quarterly*, 44(4), 301–15.

Smithers, A. and Robinson, P. (1989). *Increasing Participation in Higher Education*. London, BP Educational Service.

Sofo, F. (1990). 'Issues relating to the education of adults in the 1990s: Britain and Australia', *International Journal of University Adult Education*, 29(3), 33–54.

Spee, A. and Borman, R. (eds) (1991). *Performance Indicators in Higher Education*. Paris, OECD.

Spencer, L. and Taylor, R. (1990). 'Universities and the provision of access courses', *Adults Learning*, 2(4), 99–101.

Squires, G. (ed.) (1983) *Innovation through Recession*. Guildford, SRHE.

Squires, G. (1986). *Modularisation*. Manchester, CONTACT.

Squires, G. (1987). *Organisation and Content of Studies at the Post-Compulsory Level*. Paris, OECD.

SRHE (1983). *Excellence in Diversity. Towards a New Strategy for Higher Education*. Guildford, SRHE.

Stephens, M.D. (ed.) (1989). *University Education and the National Economy*. London, Routledge.

Stern, M.R. (1990). 'The new majority: impact of older students upon the university today', CERI/IMHE Workshop on Strategies for University Planning: Meeting the Needs of a New Clientele, Paris, OECD.

Stoddart, J. (1991). *Developments in Continuing Education – the Next Ten Years in Higher Education*. Nottingham, PACE.

Summers, N. (Chairman) (1988). *The Funding of University Extramural Departments. Report of the Official Working Party*. London, DES.

TEED (1990). *Higher Education Developments. The Skills Link*. Sheffield, TEED, Employment Department Group.

TEED (1991). *The First Year of Enterprise in Higher Education*. Sheffield, Employment Department.

Teichler, U. (1990). 'The challenge of lifelong learning for the university', *AUE Informationsdienst, Hochschule und Weiterbildung*, 2, 7–14.

Thomas, J.E. (1985). *Learning Democracy in Japan. The Social Education of Japanese Adults*. London, Sage.

Thompson, J.L. (ed.) (1980). *Adult Education for a Change*. London, Hutchinson.

Tight, M. (1991). *Higher Education: a Part-time Perspective*. Milton Keynes, Open University Press.

Tough, A. (1971). *The Adult's Learning Projects*. Toronto, OISE.

Tough, A. (1982). *Intentional Changes*. Chicago, Follett.

Training Agency (1989). *Enterprise in Higher Education*. Sheffield, Training Agency.

Trow, M. (1989). 'The Robbins trap: British attitudes and the limits of expansion', *Higher Education Quarterly*, 43(1), 55–75.

Tuckett, A. (1991). *Towards a Learning Workforce. A Policy Discussion Paper on Adult Learners at Work*. Leicester, NIACE.

UCAE (Universities Council for Adult Education) (1970). *University Adult Education in the Later Twentieth Century*, Birmingham, UCAE.

UCACE (1982). *Annual Report 1980–81*. Liverpool, UCACE.

UCACE (1990). *Annual Report 1988–89*. Leicester, UCACE.

UDACE (1989). *Understanding Learning Outcomes*. Leicester, UDACE.

UDACE (1991). *What Can Graduates Do?* Leicester, UDACE.

UFC (1989a). *The Aims of the Universities Funding Council*. London, UFC.

UFC (1989b). 'Continuing education: future funding arrangements', circular letter 15/89, London, UFC.

UFC (1989c). 'Funding and planning: 1991/92 to 1994/95', circular letter 39/89, London, UFC.

UGC (1964). *Report of the Committee on University Teaching Methods* (the Hale Report). London, HMSO.

UGC (1984a). *A Strategy for Higher Education into the 1990s. The University Grants Committee's Advice.* London, HMSO.

UGC (1984b). *Report of the Continuing Education Working Party.* London, UGC.

UK Universities (1990). 'Planning statements 1991/92–94/95' (planning statements by all UK UFC-funded universities and colleges to the UFC).

Unesco (1976). *Recommendation on the Development of Adult Education.* Paris, Unesco.

Wagner, L. (ed.) (1982). *Agenda for Institutional Change in Higher Education.* Guildford, SRHE.

Wagner, L. (1990). 'Adults in higher education: the next five years', *Adults Learning*, 2(4), 94–6.

Weil, S. and McGill, I. (eds) (1989). *Making Sense of Experiential Learning: Diversity in Theory and Practice.* Milton Keynes, Open University Press.

Willen, B. (1984). *Self-Directed Learning and Distance Education.* Uppsala, Department of Education, University of Uppsala.

Williams, G. and Blackstone, T. (1983). *Response to Adversity: Higher Education in a Harsh Climate.* Guildford, SRHE.

Williams, G. and Loder, C. (1991). 'Menage a trois', *Times Higher Education Supplement*, 28 June.

Woodley, A. *et al.* (1987). *Choosing to Learn: Adults in Education.* Milton Keynes, Open University Press.

Wright, P. (1989). 'Access or exclusion? Some comments on the history and future prospects of continuing education in England', *Studies in Higher Education*, 14(1), 23–40.

Yorke, M. (1991). *Performance Indicators.* London, CNAA.

Index

The Society for Research into Higher Education

The Society for Research into Higher Education exists to stimulate and co-ordinate research into all aspects of higher education. It aims to improve the quality of higher education through the encouragement of debate and publication on issues of policy, on the organization and management of higher education institutions, and on the curriculum and teaching methods.

The Society's income is derived from subscriptions, sales of its books and journals, conference fees and grants. It receives no subsidies, and is wholly independent. Its individual members include teachers, researchers, managers and students. Its corporate members are institutions of higher education, research institutes, professional, industrial and governmental bodies. Members are not only from the UK, but from elsewhere in Europe, from America, Canada and Australasia, and it regards its international work as amongst its most important activities.

Under the imprint SRHE & Open University Press, the Society is a specialist publisher of research, having some 30 titles in print. The Editorial Board of the Society's Imprint seeks authoritative research or study in the field. It offers competitive royalties, a highly recognizable format in both hard- and paper-back and the world-wide reputation of the Open University Press.

The Society also publishes *Studies in Higher Education* (three times a year), which is mainly concerned with academic issues, *Higher Education Quarterly* (formerly *Universities Quarterly*), mainly concerned with policy issues, *Abstracts* (three times a year), and SRHE NEWS (four times a year).

The Society holds a major annual conference in December, jointly with an institution of higher education. In 1990, the topic was 'Industry and Higher Education', at and with the University of Surrey and in 1991, 'Research and Higher Education in Europe' at and with the University of Leicester. Future conferences include in 1992, 'Learning to Effect', with Nottingham Polytechnic, and in 1993, 'Governments and the Higher Education Curriculum' with the University of Sussex. In addition it holds regular seminars and consultations on topics of current interest.

The Society's committees, study groups and branches are run by members. The groups at present include:
Teacher Education Study Group
Continuing Education Group
Staff Development Group
Excellence in Teaching & Learning
Women in Higher Education Group.

enefits to members

ndividual

Individual members receive:

- The NEWS, the Society's publications list, conference details and other material included in mailings.
- Reduced rates for *Studies in Higher Education* (£9.75 per year – full price £72) and *Higher Education Quarterly* (£12.35 per year – full price £43).
- A 35 percent discount on all Open University Press & SRHE publications.
- Free copies of the Proceedings (or Precedings) – commissioned papers on the theme of the Annual Conference.
- Free copies of *Higher Education Abstracts*.
- Reduced rates for conferences.
- Extensive contacts and scope for facilitating initiatives.
- Reduced reciprocal memberships.

Corporate

Corporate members receive:

- All benefits of individual members, plus
- Free copies of *Studies in Higher Education*.
- Unlimited copies of the Society's publications at reduced rates.
- Special rates for its members, e.g. to the Annual Conference.

Subscriptions August 1991–July 1992

Individual members

standard fee	£47
hardship (e.g. unwaged)	£22
students and retired	£14

Corporate members

a) teaching institutions		
under 1000 students	£170	
up to 3000 students	£215	
over 3000 students	£320	
b) non-teaching institutions	up to £325	
c) industrial/professional bodies	up to £325	

Further information: SRHE, 344–354 Gray's Inn Road, London, wc1x 8bp, UK. Tel: 071 837 7880
Catalogue: SRHE & Open University Press, Celtic Court, 22 Ballmoor, Buckingham mk18 1xw. Tel: (0280) 823388